What People Are Saying About
I Tried Until I Almost Died

"We've known Sandra McCollom for over half of her life, and she is the real deal—a devoted Christian, wife, and mother. In this book, she shares with honesty and openness how she learned to appropriate God's grace into her life and experience more joy. . . . Sandra's story helps us lay aside weights and encumbrances in order to be more effective in the challenges of life (Hebrews 12:1). Pondering these pages will remind you that it was for freedom that Christ set us free (Galatians 5:1). Her words will help you break away from unreasonable perfectionism and begin to excel in the mercy and love of God."

—Pastors Jeff and Patsy Perry, St. Louis Family Church
(Sandra's pastors)

"I had the privilege of personally hearing Sandra share her journey of being completely liberated by God's amazing grace. I am thrilled that you, too, can now hear her story. I have no doubt that you will experience the transformative power of knowing our wonderful Lord Jesus as you see what He has done for Sandra in her own life."

—Joseph Prince, international best-selling author of *The Power of Right Believing* and senior pastor of New Creation Church

"In this book, Sandra shares her journey of learning to walk daily in God's grace and live for His pleasure. When we discover what a wonderful, loving Father we have in God, we can experience a life filled with joy and peace. Our loving Father said, 'My grace is all you need. My power works best in weakness' (2 Corinthians 12:9). Whatever your heavy load is today, bring it to the Lord. You are His child, and He delights to care for you. May Sandra's story inspire you to draw near and trust Him today."

—James and Betty Robison, co-hosts of *LIFE Today* television

"I love Sandra McCollom and have watched the message of this book literally transform her life. As she has discovered her own belovedness, she now wants to help you discover yours. You will learn that you are already thoroughly loved and approved of by Jesus."

—CHRISTINE CAINE, founder of the A21 Campaign and best-
selling author of *Unstoppable*

"Sandra McCollom offers her readers the ultimate encouragement: God does not expect us to be perfect, and His love and grace extend to us right where we are. In a world that so often pushes us to be as close to perfect as we can, this message promising the relaxation and peace of God's unyielding grace and love cannot be missed! Sandra is truly a great woman of God with something to say. This book is a must-read."

—TOMMY BARNETT, co-pastor of Phoenix First and founder
of the Los Angeles Dream Center

"Rest is a state of being where we maintain peace. Resting in God is complete peace with assurance that we can place our faith in Him. It sounds so simple. Why then do we struggle and take on unneeded anxiety and frustrations? Sandra McCollom's book is an honest depiction of personal struggles on the matter and victories found."

—DR. MARILYN HICKEY, president and founder of Marilyn
Hickey Ministries

I TRIED
UNTIL
I ALMOST
DIED

From Anxiety & Frustration
to Rest & Relaxation

I TRIED
UNTIL
I ALMOST
DIED

SANDRA McCOLLOM
Foreword by Dave & Joyce Meyer

WATERBROOK
PRESS

I Tried Until I Almost Died
Published by WaterBrook Press
12265 Oracle Boulevard, Suite 200
Colorado Springs, Colorado 80921

Trade Paperback ISBN 978-1-60142-577-5
eBook ISBN 978-1-60142-578-2

The Cataloging-in-Publication Data is on file with the Library of Congress.

Printed in the United States of America
2015—First Edition

10 9 8 7 6 5 4 3 2 1

SPECIAL SALES
Most WaterBrook Multnomah books are available at special quantity discounts when purchased in bulk by corporations, organizations, and special-interest groups. Custom imprinting or excerpting can also be done to fit special needs. For information, please e-mail SpecialMarkets@WaterBrookMultnomah.com or call 1-800-603-7051.

To my husband, Steve, and my twin girls, Angel and Starr.
Thank you for loving and forgiving me
and letting us start over again as a family.
I love you!

Contents

Contents

Foreword by
Dave and Joyce Meyer

It is our pleasure to introduce to you our daughter Sandra McCollom and her new and exciting book on grace. First, let us say that Sandra is an excellent daughter. Out of our four children she was the easiest to raise simply because she always wanted to be good. She didn't even cry as a baby, and we took her to the doctor thinking she was too good—something had to be wrong! He assured us she was fine and encouraged us to enjoy it. Even then perfectionist tendencies must have been on the horizon of Sandra's life.

We watched Sandra suffer needlessly through her childhood and teenage years as she pressured herself to be something none of us has the ability to be: perfect. Maybe your own efforts at perfection have been similarly frustrating. Peace is not possible until we understand God's amazing grace in sending us Jesus, the perfect sacrifice, to pay for our sins and take our punishment. Grace is the only antidote for frustration, struggle, and misery.

Sandra knows firsthand what that struggle is like, but thankfully, she also knows firsthand what freedom is like. God has graciously given her a genuine revelation on the power of His grace that is available for every area of our lives. Whether we need forgiveness for sin, strength in difficult times, wisdom for parenting, or anything else you can imagine, God's grace is sufficient to meet all of our needs!

We believe anyone can benefit from reading Sandra's story and will enjoy her fresh approach to teaching grace in a practical way you can apply to your life immediately. We've witnessed for ourselves that she is transformed and, in fact, continues to change as she grows in applying grace to her own life daily. The good fruit popping out on the branches of her life is eliminating the dead leaves of fleshly works that frustrated her and left her angry at herself and life in general.

Today Sandra is excited, enthusiastic, energetic, and in love with Jesus. She loves helping people, and we feel certain you will experience that help for yourself as you read *I Tried Until I Almost Died*.

—Dave and Joyce Meyer

Acknowledgments

To Mom and Dad: Thanks so much for all your love and for being there for me through it all. You're the best!

David, Shelly, Doug, Laura, Dan, Nicol: I never fail to laugh hysterically when we're together.

Pastor Jeff and Patsy: It was such a God-ordained thing when we started coming to St. Louis Family Church in 2010. Steve, the girls, and I frequently talk about how much it feels like home.

Cally: I'm so thankful that God has allowed us to walk through this journey of grace together. You've been a lifesaver to me on so many occasions. I treasure our friendship.

Pastor Mike and Pennie: Steve and I are so grateful for you, for your guidance and counsel over the years, for being such an encouragement to us, and for your friendship.

Lisa: How thankful I am that God caused our paths to cross. Thanks for always being so supportive, for your prayers, and for your friendship.

Nancy, Katie, Kim, Eva, Renee, Linda: I appreciate you ladies so much. Thanks for letting me bounce my grace thoughts off you along my journey.

Tom: Thanks for taking a chance on me.

Steve: Thanks for believing in me and my book.

Laura: Thanks for being a genius and guiding me through this whole process.

To all those who took the time to write out your story for my book: Thank you so much. I really appreciate you.

To all my Facebook friends: In October of 2012, I started writing posts about my personal journey of grace, not knowing what to expect, but your encouragement has been amazing and unending from that day until this. I appreciate you all so much.

Part I

BREAKING
FREE

1

Prison Break

Finding Release from the Shackles of Endless Expectations

From as far back as I can remember until age forty-two, I lived in a prison—not one built of bricks and mortar, but a mental prison, locked up by legalism, rules, and regulations. I placed walls around myself in an attempt to create a place of safety and security, boundaries meant to ensure that I would never step out of line and risk failure, risk God's displeasure, risk being anything less than perfect.

Instead of feeling secure, I became consumed with a continual sense that I needed to do more, to be more, to achieve more.

Just about everything I did was driven by the belief that I *should,* I *need to,* I'd *better,* or I *must.* Rarely did I do anything because I wanted to. I read the Bible because I thought I had to or God would be upset with me. And yet if you had asked me if I was having consistent devotional time with Jesus each day because I believed I had to or because I wanted to, I would have looked at you like you were crazy. I've had a tender heart toward God ever since I was a little girl, and I was always talking about how much I loved Him, but until well into adulthood, I wasn't very good at letting Him love me.

I wonder if you have found yourself in a similar prison, trapped by the sense that you can never quite do enough or be enough to satisfy your inner drive for more. Do you live with a never-ending, guilt-inducing list of expectations? If so, perhaps you can relate to my story of years spent continually chasing after the flawless life I envisioned for myself.

RULED BY RULES

Throughout much of my adult years, if anyone had asked whether I was happy, I would have wholeheartedly replied, "Oh yes, so happy." In truth, I was anxious, unstable, and extremely fearful—but believe it or not, I didn't know it. My extreme ambition for reaching my personal goals hid the struggle going on inside me.

I rose early almost every morning to enthusiastically tackle my unrealistic mile-long list of things to accomplish. Inevitably, I would fail to complete all the items on my list, but somewhere between the end of that day and the next morning, my willpower would pick me back up off the ground and stand me up so I could try again and again and again and again. You see, I have a melancholy-sanguine personality, and the sanguine part would aid me in being positive despite my history of what I deemed to be failure. Every morning I would say (and wholeheartedly believe) "Today is going to be better than yesterday" as I imagined my list of tasks being checked off.

Today's the day I'll get this right. I'll get my act together. I'll show them, I thought. I'm not sure who I thought "them" was, but now I realize that I was desperately driven to prove to myself and to the world that I was a good Christian, a good wife, a good mother, a good daughter, a good sister, a good employee, and a good friend. Coming up short in any area of life was simply not acceptable to me. I expected peak performance at all times from myself and my family.

Rules were my particular specialty. Nearly everything in the McCollom household operated according to a rule. We must keep the house straightened at all times so Mom won't be embarrassed when people stop by. We must drink enough water or endure another speech from Mom about how water is critical to our health. We must eat healthy and have dessert only once a week because we can't give room to the flesh to want more and more. We must say "please" and "thank you," especially in front of other people so they will think well of Mom. We must place homeschool books on the kitchen table only during the day and not leave them lying around the house. We must get our schoolwork done during the day, or we will work at night too (despite the fact that flexibility is one of the reasons we chose homeschooling in the first place). We must clear our music playlist off the sound system for the next person using it; otherwise we will get a speech on the importance of being considerate of others. We must be obedient. We must put all of our Wii accessories away properly when finished. We must wipe our bathroom counter every day. And we can't forget to wipe the faucet or we will have to march back to the bathroom and do it again. We must clean the entire house every two weeks, even if it doesn't look dirty.

Oh, and friend, let me tell you, I am just getting started. This list is merely a glimpse of the many regulations that gave my world the illusion of orderliness, safety, and control and therefore ruled our days.

Looking back, I seriously do not know how anyone could have followed all my rules. I wasn't a mean wife or mother, but I was very regimented. If my girls disobeyed in something—how could they not with all those rules?—I felt they needed a consequence, period, end of conversation. After all, I had to keep up my reputation as a godly parent. Certainly there are benefits to having an orderly home, but my requirement for strict adherence to these rules left my girls in continual fear of breaking the law. We all lived in frustration. My girls felt they could never measure up, and I was tired of trying to enforce my endless rules. All of us were in desperate need of mercy, but I couldn't see beyond the boundaries and guidelines that kept me imprisoned.

And believe it or not, I placed more rules on myself than on anyone else.

For example, I obsessed about eating healthy, feeding my family healthy foods, exercising, and everything else that had to do with health. I read every label of every food item I bought and every personal care item used in our home, such as toothpaste, shampoo, and hand soap, just for starters. I spent hours on the computer to research the various ingredients used in each product so I wouldn't harm my family or myself.

The problem wasn't that I believed in eating healthy and using healthy personal care products; it was the fact that I became completely consumed with fear in this area of my life. Rather than making wise choices with the information I had and trusting God to guide me, I acted as if I alone could ensure my family's health. And yet during that time, when the products in our home probably were the healthiest they have ever been, I suffered more health problems than in all the rest of my life put together. I certainly don't believe God gave me the health problems, nor do I believe the healthy products backfired. You know what I think? I think stress consumed my life and undermined my health—the stress of trying to be perfect and perfectly in control, without considering what Jesus had accomplished for me through His finished work on the cross.

> All of us were in desperate need of mercy, but I couldn't see beyond the boundaries and guidelines that kept me imprisoned.

I was exhausted from running nonstop on my treadmill of accomplishment. I only allowed myself a break on those days when I had completed all my duties. But my rest period was brief because I didn't want to lose momentum. I had to keep going to prove to myself and everyone else that my life and my efforts were worthwhile. So I continued pushing myself, running, completely out of breath. *I . . . must . . . keep . . . going!* my mind would scream.

I even became a competitive sprinter at the age of thirty-nine. This was yet another way that I intended to prove my worth and value. I didn't care much about beating other people, but I loved trying to outrun my previously recorded time, always looking to best myself, similar to the way I would race against my list at home.

I desperately wanted to be at peace but couldn't seem to hold on to it for very long. I blamed my circumstances and my schedule. Every time someone got in the way of my plan, especially if it was nearing the end of the day and I realized every item on my list would not be checked off, I would go into a panic, running around the house in a frantic dash to get everything done, all the while throwing out negative, frustrated comments: "I feel like all I ever do is work." Well, I certainly had that right. I did not know how to find my personal worth and value in anything besides work. Or I might blurt out something like "Why do I always have to think of everything that needs to be done around here?" while judging the rest of my family for not taking the initiative I felt they should have.

After comparing notes with others, especially women, I've realized this tendency to hold others responsible for the goals we set for ourselves is all too common. Marla finds herself asking, "Why am I the only one who cares around here?" Jody described the inner dialogue like this: "It usually starts with my thinking *What have you done today?* And then I proceed to itemize the diapers I've changed, laundry I've washed and folded, the meals I've made (and cleaned up), and how many times I've swept the floor . . . all in my head." In her overwhelmed moments Carla wonders, *Why do I even bother? It's not like anyone ever notices.*

Chrissie perfectly captured the mantra that keeps so many of us under constant self-induced pressure: "If I don't do it, it won't get done." For many of us—certainly for me in the days when life was governed by my rules and regulations—the idea of something left undone is utterly unacceptable, no matter how much stress might result from persisting in the goal.

My husband, Steve, is a person who loves peace. He watched as I repeatedly grew frustrated with life, and he prayed that I would see what I was doing to myself. He tried to talk with me about it on a few occasions, but I immediately became defensive: "Well, I feel like I am really peaceful. You just don't ever see what I do right around here." Can you believe I actually had the audacity to say that? Steve couldn't see my so-called peacefulness because it wasn't real. You can tell what a trap of deception the devil had me in. I already felt so condemned by my inability to keep up with life that I simply couldn't receive any advice or correction. I couldn't take feeling any worse about myself than I already did.

Now I realize that it is a miracle of God that my husband and kids did not grow to hate me. I did have a sparkly, bubbly side, but I was all over the map emotionally. At times I felt like I hated my life, which made no sense because I have a wonderful husband and two beautiful girls. The tension in our home mounted each year as I endured almost continual self-imposed pressure and lived in a perpetual state of anxiety. I began to have health problems, including a cyst the size of a cantaloupe. I was buried under guilt and condemnation, certain that my physical trials were a punishment from God for my shortcomings.

What about you, friend? Are you tired of being buried underneath a mountain of guilt and condemnation? Are you fed up with letting your fears govern your life? Let me share with you a secret that I finally learned for myself: guilt and condemnation and trying harder will never deliver us. They will never drive us to the longed-for destination of sweet freedom. They serve only to weaken us and send us deeper into discouragement.

However, there is a way you can be set free from any and all feelings of guilt and condemnation. I know this is true because I am finally enjoying this freedom. After years of trying harder and harder, I escaped the prison that held me for so long.

It all started when I got so fed up with trying to live the Christian life the way I believed it should be lived that I came to the end of myself at last. Just a week before the end of 2011, I found myself crying out to God. *I can't live like this anymore,* I told Him. *I am so tired, God. I just can't keep up. I need serious help.*

That is exactly what He was waiting to hear!

GOD STEPS IN

After I had lived for years under my own long list of laws, the spirit of independence that drove me finally began to break and I admitted that I needed help.

It was 5:30 a.m. on January 2, 2012, according to my MacJournal. I was just beginning my devotional time. I'd never been a big proponent of New Year's resolutions, probably because, deep down inside, I knew they would just add more rules to my long-running list, more chances for me to fall short of my expectations once again. Nevertheless, that day I reluctantly asked God if there was anything in particular that He wanted me to accomplish in the year ahead.

Well, He certainly did not ask me to accomplish something else, but He did have plenty to show me that morning. I remember typing words into my MacJournal so fast I could barely keep up.

I told God that I wanted to think less and laugh more in 2012 . . . I get way too mental about things, and this year I want to live more like Jesus did.

About this time I felt the love of God absolutely wash over me like a gigantic wave. I kept typing rapidly as new thoughts and impressions poured into my heart.

I have always wanted to live more like Jesus did, full of peace and laughter, but yesterday it hit me. Jesus never hurried, and He was *not* stressed out. He was *not* in a race with Himself to see how much He could accomplish. He just lived out each day staying in close relationship with His Father and went about doing good to people!

I am getting off the accomplishment train. I am done trying to get my worth and value out of what other people think about me or even out of what I think of myself. God thinks I am special enough that He sent His only Son to die on the cross for me to save me from myself. God loves me so deeply. I receive His love. I consciously take it in right now, just like breathing. I am confident in Christ, and I believe that God is going to allow me and my family to help more people this year than we have ever been able to help before. Jesus was not in a hurry, and I should not be in a hurry. Being too busy—and therefore being in a hurry—has got to be one of the worst deceptions the devil has ever pulled on people. When we are in a hurry, we cannot hear from God, we cannot be consistently loving toward others, and we cannot accomplish what God wants us to accomplish. Oh, we may get our list checked off all right, but not necessarily God's list for the day.

As I typed all of this, I sensed a strong touch from the Holy Spirit. It felt like He was opening my eyes to so many things. The deception that had blinded me to God's love and grace began to peel away layer by layer by layer. I had to squarely face the fact that on many levels I had been living according to deluded thinking.

Some people who experience the kind of mental torment I had put myself through either were raised in legalistic homes or have sat under a lot of legalistic teaching in their churches. They've received continual messages about the "thou shalts" and "thou shalt nots" of their faith.

This was not the case with me. I grew up in a loving home with wonderful parents, and I have been privileged since childhood to be part of many really great churches. I had actually been taught early on the truth about God's grace. But somewhere along the way I placed myself under the law in an effort to please God. Nobody else was placing me under these rules and regulations. I did it to myself—and not only that, I didn't even realize I was doing it. I was consumed with fears and misconceptions about God, but He was about to show me the truth in a personal revelation of His heart toward me.

The next day as I reflected back on this whole experience and specifically on how I had spent most of my life imprisoned by my own set of rules and priorities, I repented for living like a fool in this area and then proceeded to pray these words:

God, please help me to live this year as You would have me live . . .
as Jesus would have lived if He was still here walking the earth. Help
me to drop all my expectations of myself and just plop right in the
middle of Your plan for me each day. As I start doing this, help me
not to get arrogant about it but instead help me to just glorify You!

Please help me to prepare myself and be ready to be used by You at any given moment.

I love You, and I pray this in Jesus' name.

I didn't say anything to anybody about this change in my perspective. Instead, over the next few weeks, I watched with caution as I lived in a peace that I had never known before. I was responding to everything differently, and my life lacked the frustration and anxiety that had previously been my constant companions.

One of the first personal changes I noticed after January 2 was that I stopped racing with myself. I not only got off the treadmill, I couldn't even find it anymore. It was so weird, living without trying to prove something to myself all the time. It felt absolutely wonderful! I kept thinking, *Is this real? Did God do something on January 2 that has made a permanent change in me?* I decided to keep waiting and watching.

Here is a journal entry from January 28:

Well, I obviously realize at this point that I have received an all-out *miracle* regarding the way I view and respond to life. I am so relaxed that it is unbelievable.

As the peace continued over the next several weeks, I thought, *If I don't tell Steve what's going on, why I'm no longer living at such a frantic pace, he might begin to wonder about me.* So I told him while in tears, "God has done something in me. I'm different." Then I shared with him what I just shared with you. Soon afterward, we sat down with our girls to talk about the change in my heart and how we wanted that change to impact our home.

Once God had removed the blinders from my eyes, He also helped me see down to the core of the frustrations in my relationships with my girls. He showed me that they didn't feel loved for who they were, for themselves, especially when they made mistakes. I couldn't give unconditional love because I didn't know that God loved me unconditionally. Most of the time I pictured God standing over me with this serious look, just waiting for me to mess up, and when I did, I felt I was separated from Him until I got myself "straightened out." I'd been treating my kids the same way that I believed God was treating me. But God, in His mercy and grace, has helped me restore all this, and now we are learning about His endless mercy and amazing grace together as a family every day. This does not mean I am perfect. I still make mistakes, and on some days it feels like I make them endlessly. When I do, I apologize to my girls and ask them to forgive me. We freely forgive in this family because we know we have been forgiven of much. *forgiveness*

JOIN ME ON AN INCREDIBLE JOURNEY

Beginning with that January day, the Holy Spirit began leading me on an incredible journey, teaching me to think differently about how He thinks of me! I felt like Job, who said, "I had heard of You [only] by the hearing of the ear, but now my [spiritual] eye sees You" (42:5, AMP). The Holy Spirit helped me—and continues to help me—to see the truth about God as a heart-shaping revelation instead of as head knowledge only.

Through His Word and through the biblical teaching of others, God began to reveal to me that I had been living under the law instead of under His grace. Over the next twelve months God radically transformed my thinking and my believing, which in turn transformed my life, my marriage, my parenting, my friendships—not to mention my list of expectations.

I had a critical, destiny-changing moment while reading Joyce Meyer's book *Do Yourself a Favor . . . Forgive*. Although Joyce is my mom and I'd heard these truths from her before, this time as I read them, God spoke to my heart and I finally understood that I was really angry at myself for not living up to my own expectations of me. As I've explained, previously when I got to the end of each day, I would see only the things that were left on my list, undone. I didn't celebrate the things I had accomplished. I was an all-or-nothing person. I still remember the day, a few weeks after my incredible experience with God on January 2, when I decided to forgive myself for not living up to my own expectations.

For so long I'd been trying to be perfect in order to please God, not understanding why I seemed unable to measure up. But God opened my eyes to the beauty of grace, to the truth "that we are utterly incapable of living the glorious lives God wills for us, [so] God did it for us. Out of sheer generosity he put us in right standing with himself. A pure gift" (Romans 3:23–24, MSG).

As I have come to understand this precious gift over the past few years, here's what I have learned: grace is God's undeserved, unmerited, unearned favor. When we receive God's grace by faith, it produces His divine empowerment in our lives. But it is important to remember that this empowerment comes from Jesus alone, not us. True grace never arises from our personal work. Paul, the greatest apostle of grace, described this truth clearly in Romans 11:6: "And if by grace, then it is no longer of works; otherwise grace is no longer grace. But if it is of works, it is no longer grace; otherwise work is no longer work" (NKJV). True grace always points us back to Jesus and what He has done, not to ourselves or anything we have to do. Grace makes us Jesus-conscious instead of self-conscious![1]

> For so long I'd been trying to be perfect in order to please God, not understanding why I seemed unable to measure up. But God opened my eyes to the beauty of grace.

No wonder I'd been so exhausted and frustrated. For years I'd refused the gift of grace and tried to approach God based on my own strength and merit. First Peter 5:5 says that God frustrates the proud but gives grace to the humble. As He removed the blinders from my eyes, I became less and less occupied with my own good behavior and self-efforts and increasingly occupied with Christ—and "the grace of our Lord was poured out on me abundantly, along with the faith and love that are in Christ Jesus" (1 Timothy 1:14, NIV).

Everything is different now, under grace. Living this way, my desire for Him is so strong. I have fallen more in love with Jesus than I ever imagined possible. The word *Savior* has taken on a whole new meaning for me! Do you recall that in my journal entry I made a decision to consciously take in God's love, just like breathing? That practice continues to this very day. Receiving His love has become just as real and easy to me as breathing.

As I began to learn the truth about grace, I also developed an insatiable desire to study the Bible. I still can't get enough! When it is time for bed, I find myself wishing it was time to get up so I can spend more time with Him as I study His Word. After God unspooled my faulty thinking and spooled it up correctly, I started reading the Bible with brand-new eyes. The Holy Spirit first led me to read the book of John, specifically paying special attention to the words of Jesus. I couldn't believe what I was reading. In the very same verses where I'd always seen a spiritual to-do list, I was now seeing the gift of grace, an invitation to rest in His strength alone!

Here's an example: John 8:36 says, "So if the Son liberates you [makes you free men], then you are really and unquestionably free" (AMP). I had read this verse so many times before, but this year a light came on. "Oh, I see," I said out loud. "If Jesus sets me free, then I am *really* free, whereas even if my own efforts appear to have set me free, I am *not really* free."

God wanted me to know that I didn't have to continually prove myself to Him—or to others. He showed me that I'd been propping up my self-worth with a long list of things. Proverbs 3:5 says, "Lean on, trust in, and be confident in the Lord" (AMP). Oh, what a relief to think of leaning on His everlasting arms instead of chasing my never-ending list. I knew this was not a current description of my life, but it was where God wanted me to end up. It was His goal for me.

And it's His goal for you!

Maybe you've begun to realize that too many of your days are spent chasing after security and self-worth, pursuing props to bolster your sense of value. Money, possessions, family, beauty, physical fitness, career, titles, awards, diplomas, intelligence, humor, self-righteousness, past victories, accomplishments, traditions, trends, having a perfectly clean house all the time, having your to-do list completely checked off, having the good opinion of others—all these and more can consume our attention and rob us of the freedom that comes from resting in God's grace.

As I came to a deeper understanding of God's love for me, He began to show me that I was propped up by several things on the list above, most especially other people's good opinions. I would feel this pain in my gut when I didn't receive outward displays of encouragement, even something as simple as not getting a thank-you for showing kindness toward someone. Certainly, there is nothing wrong with wanting to be encouraged as long as we don't start depending on people for this or get angry when they don't come through for us.

I realized that God already has placed His own stamp of approval on us. "He anointed us, set his seal of ownership on us, and put his Spirit in our hearts as a deposit, guaranteeing what is to come" (2 Corinthians 1:21–22, NIV). Although it was a painful process to work through, God did me a favor when He helped me anchor my security in Christ alone. True freedom comes in knowing that we are loved by God, unconditionally. Our confidence, our worth, our value do not rest on the response of others or on what we accomplish today but are established firmly on Christ alone.

Maybe you, like me, received your salvation by grace, but then started trying to do the rest of the Christian life on your own in an effort to please God. If so, in the pages that follow, I want to share with you the freedom I've found and the joy that can be yours—simply by choosing to rest in God's amazing grace.

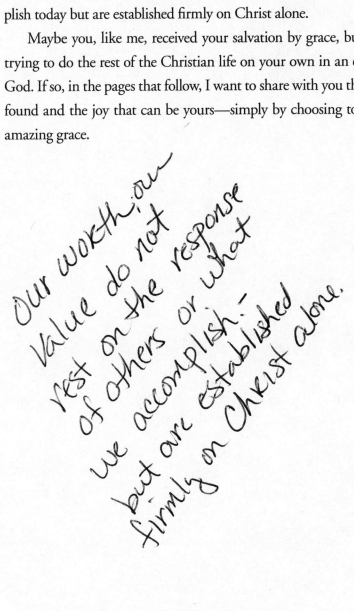

2

When We Come to the End of Ourselves

How the Promise of Grace Brings Rest to Our Weary Souls

Friend, do you find yourself wondering if you have done enough for God? Are you looking for a to-do list to accomplish for God in order to be acceptable to Him? When you struggle with sin, do you think you would be able to overcome if you would just try harder? Are you having a hard time fighting off guilt and condemnation after you sin? Are you afraid that God will be mad at you if you don't read the Bible, pray, or serve? Would you feel safer if someone just gave you a list of rules and said "Follow these and you will be okay," as opposed to your being led by the Spirit?

Just a few short years ago—and for most of my life—my own answer to all of these questions would have been a resounding Y-E-S! What was I missing? Grace. My hope did not rest in simply receiving God's unmerited favor (grace) but in my being able to do all the right things to earn it. I had heard the word *grace* over the years, but because I was trying to live the Christian life under the law, my legalistic brain rejected grace as rapidly as a machine gun spits out bullets. My brain never gave grace a chance because, in my mind, I had it covered as long as I followed the rules.

Thankfully, when God stepped in on January 2, 2012, He gave me a brand-new start to a brand-new life. Instead of picturing God watching my every move and waiting to catch me in a mistake, I began to read the Bible with new eyes and to see God as my heavenly Father, the One who loves me unconditionally and has already declared me chosen, holy, and dearly loved (see Colossians 3:12, NIV).

STOP THE CRAZINESS

One of the most fascinating places God led me to in the Bible as part of my journey into grace was Galatians 3. I remember reading the entire chapter one day, then just bawling my eyes out—not because I was sad but because I was starting to see more clearly just what had held me in bondage for so many years. As the light of grace dawned on my weary soul, I experienced a new level of relief, beyond words.

Here's how the chapter opens, with the apostle Paul addressing believers who, like me, acted as if they could earn God's favor:

> You crazy Galatians! Did someone put a hex on you? Have you taken leave of your senses? Something crazy has happened, for it's obvious that you no longer have the crucified Jesus in clear focus in your lives. His sacrifice on the cross was certainly set before you clearly enough. (verse 1, MSG)

Definitely, someone had cast a spell over me—and it was the devil. He had me trapped into thinking that I had to work constantly to stay on God's good side. As I moved further into this passage, I began to feel like the apostle Paul had been reading my mind.

> Let me put this question to you: How did your new life begin? Was it by working your heads off to please God? Or was it by responding to God's Message to you? Are you going to continue this craziness? For only crazy people would think they could complete by their own efforts what was begun by God. If you weren't smart enough or strong enough to begin it, how do you suppose you could perfect it? Did you go through this whole painful learning process for nothing? It is not yet a total loss, but it certainly will be if you keep this up! (verses 2–4, MSG)

As I read these words, I sobbed in recognition. *This is exactly what I have been doing,* I realized. *I have been on a works trip, relying not on God, Jesus, and the Holy Spirit but on me, myself, and I.* I started out right, receiving salvation by grace at the age of eight, but somewhere along the line I had adopted a set of rules I believed I must follow to earn God's pleasure.

> Answer this question: Does the God who lavishly provides you with his own presence, his Holy Spirit, working things in your lives you could never do for yourselves, does he do these things because of your strenuous moral striving *or* because you trust him to do them in you? Don't these things happen among you just as they happened with Abraham? He believed God, and that act of belief was turned into a life that was right with God. (verses 5–6, MSG)

I couldn't believe my eyes when I read these verses. My part in this unbelievable deal—this amazing privilege of living in friendship with the Almighty—was simply to believe God just as Abraham had. Seriously?

Oh, I had complicated Christianity so much. These verses were such good news because all of my strenuous moral striving did not help me to be a better person—at least not with any consistency; instead, my efforts resulted in a lot of frustration, for me and those around me. The more I tried to be like Jesus, the more I lost my temper, felt inadequate, and experienced anxiety.

On the rare occasions when I would squeak out a little victory—maybe I didn't lose my temper for a whole week or I arrived on time three places in a row (being late was a real issue for me)—I would begin to inform others about what method I used to get free in these areas or brag about how I finally got enough discipline to "do it right." I seriously do not remember giving God the glory when I gained ground in an area of struggle. I would instead point everyone's attention back to me and what I did. Since I had trusted in myself to get the victory, I would give myself the glory.

I measured my value by what little good I accomplished, so I couldn't resist giving myself credit in front of others.

Thankfully, God's grace was showing me a new way to live! As the Holy Spirit continued to walk me through this journey, He opened my eyes to all the ways in which I had placed my trust in myself instead of in Jesus. He had me backtrack and step away from any projects I had started in my own strength and with impure motives. In several cases I had already shared my good intentions with other people, including my accountability partners and even our pastors. So I had to go back to those individuals, humble myself, tell them about the new revelation God had brought into my life, and explain that, in light of this, I was retracting my commitments to many self-appointed endeavors.

What a difference it made to recognize that all the pressure I felt was not coming from God; He wanted to free me from all that!

THE FAILURE OF SELF-EFFORT

The apostle Paul expressed clearly the problem we all face when we grasp at spiritual success through our own desperate efforts rather than simply embracing the promises and redemptive power of God:

> Is it not obvious to you that persons who put their trust in Christ
> (not persons who put their trust in the law!) are like Abraham:
> children of faith? It was all laid out beforehand in Scripture that
> God would set things right with non-Jews by *faith*. Scripture
> anticipated this in the promise to Abraham: "All nations will be
> blessed in you."
>
> So those now who live by faith are blessed along with Abraham,
> who lived by faith—this is no new doctrine! *And that means that
> anyone who tries to live by his own effort, independent of God, is
> doomed to failure.* Scripture backs this up: "Utterly cursed is every
> person who fails to carry out every detail written in the Book of the
> law." (Galatians 3:7–10, MSG)

Did you note the sentence I emphasized? Do the words "doomed to failure" stand out for you as they did for me? The light was really starting to come on now. No wonder I'd been experiencing almost continual anxiety and frustration. I was trying to live by my own effort, independent of God, and believe me, I felt like a failure.

You see, for years I'd never felt assured of how God viewed me. In my mind I was in and out, in and out: in God's good graces when I was perfectly obedient and accomplishing all that I felt I should, but out of God's good graces when I came up short. This continual swinging between acceptance and condemnation left me insecure, to say the least. Here's what Paul had to say about the situation:

> The obvious impossibility of carrying out such a moral program should make it plain that no one can sustain a relationship with God that way. The person who lives in right relationship with God does it by embracing what God arranges for him. Doing things for God is the opposite of entering into what God does for you. Habakkuk had it right: "The person who believes God, is set right by God—and that's the real life." Rule-keeping does not naturally evolve into living by faith, but only perpetuates itself in more and more rule-keeping, a fact observed in Scripture: "The one who does these things [rule-keeping] continues to live by them." (verses 11–12, MSG)

It took me many, many years before I saw that all the trying in the world was not achieving the results I wanted. I had to come to the end of myself and give up all my self-efforts, throw myself on the grace of God, and let Him take over. Now that I had done so, God's grace was carrying me to a place of assurance, a place where I would learn not to focus on what I do or don't do; instead I could trust fully and rest securely on what Jesus has already accomplished through the finished work of the cross. I was starting to absorb the incredible truth that Jesus' finished work on the cross has accomplished for me everything I will ever need. I cannot do anything apart from Him (see John 15), and when I fail, He has already paid the price for me in full.

All I needed to do was to take hold of this promise and believe it.

In John 8:12 Jesus declared, "I am the light of the world. If you follow me, you won't have to walk in darkness, because you will have the light that leads to life." Notice that He didn't instruct us to follow the law; He said, "Follow me." Being occupied with Christ—placing our trust wholly and solely in Him—leads us out of the darkness of sin and self-effort and gives us confidence to step forward into the glorious light of life in Him.

> Christ redeemed us from that self-defeating, cursed life by absorbing it completely into himself. Do you remember the Scripture that says, "Cursed is everyone who hangs on a tree"? That is what happened when Jesus was nailed to the cross: He became a curse, and at the same time dissolved the curse. And now, because of that, the air is cleared and we can see that Abraham's blessing is present and available for non-Jews, too. We are *all* able to receive God's life, his Spirit, in and with us by believing—just the way Abraham received it. (Galatians 3:13–14, MSG)

See, right here in verse 13 it says that Jesus "redeemed us from that self-defeating, cursed life by absorbing it completely." He took our failures onto Himself!

When I first started getting this revelation on the grace of God, I thought, *It can't be this easy. There must be something I need to do.* Well, it certainly wasn't easy for Jesus to hang on that cross as a curse on our behalf, but He did it for His Father and for all of us because He loved us that much. And we dishonor Him when we try to substitute our pathetic efforts for His perfect sacrifice.

> All the trying in the world was not achieving the results I wanted. I had to come to the end of myself and give up all my self-efforts, throw myself on the grace of God, and let Him take over.

You may say, "No, I would never dishonor Jesus." I would have said the same, and yet that's exactly what I was doing—for years. Every time I tried to pay for my own sins through bearing a burden of guilt and condemnation, I was, in essence, saying, "Jesus, You didn't do a good enough job on the cross, so here, let me just add in some of my self-condemnation with Your sacrifice to make sure I'm covered." Honestly, I am having a hard time writing this because I am so choked up thinking about the years that I disregarded what Jesus accomplished on my behalf. I am thankful for the mercy of God, and I don't feel guilty because I know I am forgiven. But, oh, how I want to spare others the misery that I lived in through trying in my own strength.

Consider what Jesus said to the Pharisees in John 8:24: "That is why I told you that you will die in (under the curse of) your sins; for if you do not believe that I am He [Whom I claim to be—if you do not adhere to, trust in, and rely on Me], you will die in your sins" (AMP).

In other words, these conscientious religious men who lived strictly under the law would die in their sins if they did not believe in Him. The same is true for us in any area of life where we rely on our own efforts instead of trusting in and believing on Him. When we attempt to do things in our own power, we live under a curse—the curse of continually striving and not being able to enter His rest.

But we don't have to live this way. The blood of Jesus has provided for us a new way called the New Covenant—and we are living in it right now. We can choose to trust in Jesus and His incredible love, already proven on the cross!

KEEPING THE CROSS AT THE CENTER

My friend Judy graciously shared with me her story of discovering the power of grace after having missed the point for years:

When I got saved, I wanted to do everything right—to be the best Christian I could be to make up for what Jesus had gone through on the cross. I thought, *If He did this for me, I'm going to spend the rest of my life doing things for Him.* Which is all fine and good, but I missed the point of grace.

In every area where God had given me opportunity, I wanted to be the very best, to honor those opportunities with excellence. Early on I learned that I couldn't control anyone else's behavior, so I became incredibly hard on myself. "Failure is not an option" could very well have been my mantra. *Grace* was a word in my Christian vocabulary, but I applied it mostly like a seasoning in my prayers for others. For example, I'd pray for grace and peace for someone struggling with a decision, or grace and strength for someone who had a busy schedule. Meanwhile, I spent years earning accolades, achievements, degrees, and approval. I viewed these things as a sort of a measure of how I was doing. I applied this same formula to my relationship (if you want to call it that) with Christ. When I had done it all right, I could enjoy or rest in the presence of God. The problem with my formula was that I never did it all right. I knew there were things I could do better: pray more, study more, get agitated less often, volunteer more often, and so on, ad infinitum. I could never measure up.

Several years ago, I found myself unable to keep up with the needs of my children, my husband, my seriously ill mother, and my full-time job as a licensed clinical social worker. In addition, I had been diagnosed with a chronic health problem, rheumatoid arthritis.

I knew that God was calling me home to take care of my family and myself, so I tried to work with my supervisor to scale back my hours. But due to multiple health crises with my mom, this plan wasn't successful. Soon afterward, I found myself without paid employment for the first time since I was thirteen years old—and essentially without any external means of justifying or affirming my performance.

I became quite depressed, convinced I had failed as a wife, a mom, a daughter, a friend, a social worker, and most of all as a Christian.

Then a friend shared with me a book about grace. I accepted it despite thinking, *I'm sure I've heard all this before.* But it was the right time for the Holy Spirit to reveal to me what I had been missing. Oh my! I don't know when I had forgotten how much Jesus loves me, or if I had ever truly known. Once I got a glimpse of His love and understood His grace, even in the most basic and simple way, I stopped trying to earn His favor. It was unnerving and liberating at the same time.

Even though I'd been saved for years, I had to learn that nothing I do makes me right with God. Nothing I do will make Him love me more. Christ did all of that on the cross. It is hard to believe but so freeing. All the pressure is now off me to perform, and fear of failure no longer drives me to achieve. Instead, I can now act out of my love for Him, in response to Him.

To say this revelation was transformative would be an understatement. I now pray differently; because I know He loves me and He covers me, I can be completely genuine with Him. I interact differently; I know that the grace I receive I can extend to others. In short, I am a different woman.

Yes, I still love to have a plan and a backup plan, but I'm okay if God takes over my day and my plans are disregarded. His plans are better than mine (His ways are better than mine). At the center of my life now is what Christ accomplished on the cross. His love and grace are real and available to me in every moment in every day; and this love and grace empower me to live for Him. My life is His, and it is my fervent hope and prayer that through His Spirit and grace, others see Him in my life.

I *love* that story! Can't you just feel the joy that now fills Judy's life and the freedom that guides her days? This is exactly the gift of grace that God longs for each of us to know, to embrace, and to make the hallmark of our lives.

GOD'S UNSHAKABLE, UNCONDITIONAL, PERSONAL LOVE

God desires that we get His unconditional love toward us settled firmly in our hearts and continually return to that as our place of refuge whenever we're tempted to believe we have to do something more in order to merit His favor.

When we rest our hope in His love for us, our perspective on everything changes. I don't think I would be exaggerating to say that finally recognizing God's love for me has touched almost every aspect of my life in a positive way. The "for me" part is important. Almost everybody says they know God loves people, but there is a difference between knowing that He loves people in general and knowing without a shadow of a doubt that God loves you and me individually and personally, even with all our imperfections.

God cares about everything that concerns us, and I mean everything. He even cares about that hangnail that is bothering you. His love is so personal. He loves it when we open up and talk to Him about anything, good or bad! You can thank Him for helping you get that promotion at work, but you also can open up to Him about how angry you feel when your supposed best friend shares confidential information about you with others. He is not interested in one more than the other. He doesn't prefer hearing about your victories rather than your struggles. He's interested in your whole story. God loves you very much and wants in on your whole life, every second of it.

I encourage you to reflect on God's love for you, personally, every single day. Say out loud to yourself, "God loves me, [insert your name], in a very personal way, and He is with me today." Meditate on this truth, daydream about it, become consumed with it.

> God desires that we get His unconditional love toward us settled firmly in our hearts and continually return to that as our place of refuge.

God is with you, God is on your side, and God is for you. God wanted so deeply to be in close relationship with you that He watched His only Son suffer and die to make this possible, and because of Jesus, He will never be against you. In fact, nothing in all creation will ever be able to separate you from the love of God that is revealed in Christ Jesus our Lord (see Romans 8:39).

As this truth truly takes root in your heart, it will inevitably transform you. No matter what life throws at you, your natural reaction will be to run back to the same unshakable reality: how special you are to God, how deeply He cares for you, the fact that He is with you, and the life-changing revelation that His love isn't going anywhere. You will actually start feeling that you are hidden in His love (see Colossians 3:3).

3

We've Been Looking
at It All Wrong

When We Truly Believe
in Grace, Everything Changes

One of the biggest things I've learned so far in my journey into grace is that many of the problems I thought I had actually were just wrong mind-sets toward my situation. For instance, it used to be that I couldn't get through my daily schedule without becoming frequently frustrated. Very rarely did I get through my entire list of daily tasks, and in fact, most days I struggled to get just some of them accomplished. My mind-set was "I am a failure." The problem was never my schedule to begin with, but you sure wouldn't have been able to convince me of this at the time.

Then God gave me the new mind-set that I could trust in His grace, His unmerited favor, in regard to my schedule and that, in Jesus, I am a success no matter how few or how many items I check off my to-do list on any given day. I no longer worry if my plans are thrown off course. In fact, I've been utterly amazed by the increased productivity in my life since the day He changed me. I don't think I would be exaggerating to say I get twice as much accomplished now in peace than I did when I was working myself to exhaustion with anxiety and frustration. Sometimes at the end of the day I walk around shaking my head, astonished that by His grace so much has been accomplished. It's amazing! I am not even the least bit tempted to give myself credit because I know firsthand what my life was like for so many years.

There is no answer for this unbelievable change other than the grace of God. For this reason, I continue daily, hourly, even moment by moment, if needed, to place whatever comes up in my life, expected or unexpected, under His grace. He always comes through. Certainly, sometimes I do not get my plan accomplished, but since my plan is now submitted to God's plan, He helps me accomplish everything that *He wants done* by the time it has to be done. The best part is, I get to remain at rest and watch the Master work it out! It's just as we read in John 6:28–29:

> They then said, What are we to do, that we may [habitually] be
> working the works of God? [What are we to do to carry out what
> God requires?]
>
> Jesus replied, This is the work (service) that God asks of you: that
> you believe in the One Whom He has sent [that you cleave to, trust,
> rely on, and have faith in His Messenger]. (AMP)

What matters is not how much we get done each day but that we are "working the works of God"—and to do that we simply have to rely on Jesus. What a liberating truth!

RIGHT BELIEVING MAKES ALL THE DIFFERENCE

While on this journey of grace, I read a powerful statement in Joseph Prince's book *Unmerited Favor:* "Right believing always leads to right living."[2] This has proven true not only in my life, but also in the lives of my husband, Steve, our kids, and many of our friends. When we stop believing that everything depends on us and what we do and instead begin believing in Jesus and what He has done for us, it completely changes the way we live.

At first, it seemed wrong that my part in the New Covenant was simply to believe. But then I realized that Jesus Himself said, "This is the only work God wants from you: Believe in the one he has sent" (John 6:29).

So what are we to believe about Jesus?

Believe in the finished work of the Cross (see Isaiah 53).
Believe He loves you (see Ephesians 2:4–5).
Believe your sins are forgiven, past, present, and future
(see Hebrews 10:17–18).

Believe He will never leave you or abandon you (see Hebrews 13:5).
Believe you are righteous in Christ (see Romans 3:24).
Believe He is not mad at you (see John 3:17).
Believe in His goodness (see James 1:17–18).

Believe you are protected (see Psalm 91:9–12).
Believe He is your redeemer (see Matthew 1:21).
Believe you have a new nature (see 2 Corinthians 5:17).
Believe you can do all things through Christ
(see Philippians 4:13).

Believe He is merciful (see 1 Peter 1:3).
Believe He remembers your sins no more (see Hebrews 8:12).
Believe that with God all things are possible (see Mark 10:27).
Believe He is working everything out for the good
by taking those lemons life just threw at
you and turning them into lemon meringue
pie (see Romans 8:28).

No matter what, keep believing (see Mark 5:36).

As you choose to meditate on these expressions of God's grace rather than focus on rules, you will find yourself falling more deeply in love with Jesus and you'll begin to witness the miracle of His grace changing your "have to" into a "want to." Reading the Bible becomes an adventure because you no longer see it as a manual of rules but as a book that reveals the beauty of Jesus and His promises from beginning to end. You delight in hanging out with your heavenly Father because you now understand that He loves you just because you are His son or daughter, not because of your performance. You naturally begin to take on an attitude of loving, serving, giving, and obedience. But now, instead of trying to produce obedience in your own strength in order to be in God's good graces, your submission flows from a heart convinced of God's grace.

> When we stop believing that everything depends on us and what we do and instead begin believing in Jesus and what He has done for us, it completely changes the way we live.

On the other side of grace, everything looks different.

For so long my focus had been on demonstrating good behavior, and yet all my efforts produced only minimal spiritual fruit. My outward behavior modification did not lead to inward heart transformation. But when my family and I finally got the message to stop focusing on our own behavior and start focusing instead on right believing, it was like we experienced a miracle. The Holy Spirit went to work inside us to produce amazing spiritual fruit in our lives and continues to do so to this day.

I used to lose my temper frequently, despite years of trying to get it under control. When I stopped trying to change myself and, instead of feeling guilty, began receiving God's grace (His unmerited favor), He replaced my anger with an abiding sense of peace. Now I hardly ever lose my temper! My husband's worries—about financial security, about providing for our family—have melted away under the power of God's grace as he has learned to find his security in Christ. And my girls have learned to relax in God's love and their behavior has improved without my constant reminders, now that they know they are good girls in Jesus, completely apart from their behavior.

Am I suggesting that we can just behave however we want—with no concern for the consequences? No, I'm talking about God's power transforming us as we continue to believe in and receive His unmerited favor in every situation. We have to get it straight in our heads and settled in our hearts that grace is getting something we don't deserve; therefore, we could never do enough good deeds to earn our way into His favor or do enough wrong things to undo His gift of grace!

The key here is not whether our behavior is good or bad; it's about what we believe. It takes faith to humbly accept the love, forgiveness, mercy, and righteousness in Christ offered to us through His finished work. Remember my friend Judy, who shared her story in the previous chapter? She described how she kept trying to pay God back for His grace but found out she couldn't do it. None of us can. Grace is always and only a gift of God, freely given to us. When we decide simply to receive this amazing grace and keep thanking Jesus for it, we find God's empowerment entering the scene, helping us to live lives of obedience.

Yes, Philippians 2 does talk about being obedient to God, but look at verse 13 in the Amplified Bible:

[Not in your own strength] for it is God Who is all the while effectually at work in you [energizing and creating in you the power and desire], both to will and to work for His good pleasure and satisfaction and delight.

Wow! God is the One who gives us the "want to" in the area of obedience as we start believing right. This is so true. We have absolutely experienced this. I call it the miracle of grace!

As you believe, He changes you by birthing in you the desire to walk in the Spirit. The Bible says if you are guided by the Spirit you won't obey your selfish desires (see Galatians 5:16). As we receive strength from Jesus, His power and discipline will shine through us. But we always have to remember that it is Christ living His life through us; therefore, our confidence is placed not in our discipline or willpower, but in His power.

READING THE BIBLE
THROUGH THE LENS OF GRACE

The entire Bible is filled with the good news of God's grace, but I didn't see it for years. Before I got a real understanding of God's grace, I would read each verse of the Bible thinking to myself, *What rule is there for me to follow in this verse?* My whole goal was to improve my system for earning my way into God's presence: "Just tell me the rule so I can do it and be pleasing to God." Legalism completely blinded me to the true riches of the Bible. Now that I am reading through the lens of grace, I read familiar passages and realize they don't say what I thought they did. I think, *How in the world did I get that out of reading this verse before? It doesn't say that at all.* In contrast to how legalism blinded me before, my grace glasses now help me see the Bible more clearly. Now I can treasure God's words for the truth they hold: the good news of God's grace.

For an example of what I mean, let's look together at a group of verses in

Colossians 1 that are particularly packed with grace power and contrast the old way of thinking under legalism with the new way of believing in the gospel of grace. You'll want to pay special attention to the italicized sentences as I contrast my old way of thinking with my new way of believing.

> We always pray for you, and we give thanks to God, the Father of our Lord Jesus Christ. *For we have heard of your faith in Christ Jesus and your love for all of God's people, which come from your confident hope of what God has reserved for you in heaven.* You have had this expectation ever since you first heard the truth of the Good News. (verses 3–5)

- Old Way of Thinking: My love walk comes from trying harder to be more loving.

Now I ask, "How could I have gotten that out of the italicized portion?"

- **New Way of Believing: My love walk comes from my confident hope in God's love for me!**

I've found this to be a much better way to live!

> This same Good News that came to you is going out all over the world. *It is bearing fruit everywhere by changing lives, just as it changed your lives from the day you first heard and understood the truth about God's wonderful grace.* (verse 6)

- Old Way of Thinking: Following all the rules perfectly will result in people having better lives.
- **New Way of Believing: Hearing and understanding the truth about God's wonderful grace results in changed lives!**

So we have not stopped praying for you since we first heard about you. *We ask God to give you complete knowledge of his will and to give you spiritual wisdom and understanding. Then the way you live will always honor and please the Lord, and your lives will produce every kind of good fruit. All the while, you will grow as you learn to know God better and better.* (verses 9–10)

- Old Way of Thinking: I have to produce good spiritual fruit or God will be mad at me.
- **New Way of Believing: Getting to know God better and better through a knowledge of His will, spiritual wisdom, and understanding produces people who honor and please the Lord and whose lives produce good fruit!**

We also pray that you will be strengthened with all his glorious power so you will have all the endurance and patience you need. May you be filled with joy, always thanking the Father. He has enabled you to share in the inheritance that belongs to his people, who live in the light. For he has rescued us from the kingdom of darkness and transferred us into the Kingdom of his dear Son, who purchased our freedom and forgave our sins. (verses 11–14)

- Old Way of Thinking: Having more willpower and discipline will provide me with the endurance and patience I need.
- **New Way of Believing: Receiving strength from Jesus will provide me with the endurance and patience I need!**

———

For God in all his fullness was pleased to live in Christ, and through him God reconciled everything to himself. He made peace with everything in heaven and on earth by means of Christ's blood on the cross. This includes you who were once far away from God. You were his enemies, separated from him by your evil thoughts and actions. *Yet now he has reconciled you to himself through the death of Christ in his physical body. As a result, he has brought you into his own presence, and you are holy and blameless as you stand before him without a single fault.* (verses 19–22)

- Old Way of Thinking: I can come into God's presence when I am obedient but not when I have sinned. God is pleased with me only when I am good.
- **New Way of Believing: God reconciled us through Jesus so we stand before Him, holy and blameless without a single fault because we are in Christ!**

———

But you must continue to believe this truth and stand firmly in it. Don't drift away from the assurance you received when you heard the Good News. The Good News has been preached all over the world, and I, Paul, have been appointed as God's servant to proclaim it. (verse 23)

- Old Way of Thinking: Review the rules constantly to be sure you're in full compliance.
- **New Way of Believing: Continually stand firm in the good news of grace.**

No wonder I love reading the Bible now!

WE'RE ALREADY RIGHTEOUS

In each example above, you may have noticed that my old way of thinking depended on my self-efforts. This is why I felt so anxious and frustrated a majority of the time; I knew I was coming up short. But the new way of believing depends solely on God's grace. This is why I feel so relaxed. I know God's grace is never going to change! The key, as we saw in Colossians 1:23, is to continue to believe the truth about grace and not lose the assurance we gained when we first heard the good news.

The work Jesus finished on the cross holds all the power we need to live a victorious life. Colossians 2:15 says this about Jesus: "He defeated the rulers and powers of the spiritual world. With the cross he won the victory over them and led them away, as defeated and powerless prisoners for the whole world to see" (ERV).

> The work Jesus finished on the cross holds all the power we need to live a victorious life.

Friend, isn't that awesome news? Jesus has stripped the devil of his authority over you! The devil tries everything he can think of to distract us and take our focus off this truth. In fact, lying is his specialty. In John 8:44 Jesus said the devil is the father of lies and there is no truth in him. He will never stop lying to us until that glorious day when Jesus shuts his mouth for good (see Revelation 20:10). But you can stop his attempts to deceive you by purposely and continually reminding yourself that the devil doesn't have any say in your life. Because of Jesus, he doesn't get to vote. In fact, "in all these things we overwhelmingly conquer through Him who loved us" (Romans 8:37, NASB).

The more your mind is filled with right believing, the more you'll see how simple it is to live in the power of the finished work of the Cross!

Part II

LIVING FREE

4

Trying Harder Is Not the Answer

The Grace-Led Life Gives Us Victory over Sin

S ome time ago, over a span of several years, I made a number of decisions that were not rooted in wisdom. In each instance I knew deep down in my heart that they weren't right, but I moved forward anyway. One of the decisions then led to several more wrong decisions, and for years I carried a heavy guilt load over my bad choices. I remember at least once a day I would be shaking my head in disgust with myself. I guess you could say in each scenario I felt as if I had ruined God's plan A for me in that area with my wrong choice.

After I started getting a revelation of how powerfully important my believing is, I made another decision—and this time it was a good one. I chose to believe in God's power to redeem my messes. I remember praying, *God, even though I feel like I have altered Your original plan for me in these areas by making some bad choices, I believe that You are redeeming each one of these situations so plan B can work out better than plan A ever would have. In Jesus' name I pray, amen.*

You may say, "Wow, Sandra. That was bold. Did you really think God would do that for you after what you had done?" I knew He would—and He has. In every single one of these situations, God, my awesome heavenly Father, has caused things to work out better than they were even prior to my wrong choices. That's the kind of God we serve. He can redeem anything!

WHEN WE JUST CAN'T GET IT RIGHT

Have you ever wondered why you can't seem to live a holy life no matter how hard you try? Have you been trying to solve the "you" problem for a long time? No matter how much you want to do the right thing, for some reason you can't seem to consistently carry it out? *F r u s t r a t i n g.*

Even apart from the spiritual aspects of life, perhaps you feel as if you're always failing. I know I did. I'd get up early, try to be positive, then fly from thing to thing, trying to get through the mile-long list of expectations I had placed upon myself the second I put my feet on the floor that morning. As I hit unexpected hurdles and fell farther behind, I'd grow increasingly discouraged and impatient with myself and others. Panic began to rise up within me as I realized that, once again, I was failing to live up to my expectations. Mentally and physically, I was running in all directions, almost hyperventilating, while thinking, *I have to get this stuff done. How am I going to get it done? Oh my goodness, it's not going to get done.*

Just as right believing leads us to right living, so wrong believing leads us to wrong living. "I am a failure" was the wrong belief that drove my panic, then led to undesirable words and actions. I would sometimes start barking out orders to my family as I spotted everything my kids had left lying around the house, and after that I would decide my husband wasn't giving me enough encouragement. And on and on. I might continue in my frenzied efforts for anywhere from a minute to a whole hour, but eventually I would just about collapse under condemnation. Not only was I burdened with guilt over my uncompleted checklist, but now even more guilt was stacked on top of that for my lack of self-control and unloving attitude toward my family. Lots of times the whirlwind of striving culminated in a crying session because I felt so terrible about myself.

Now, just to clarify, my fearful attitude didn't play out in mistreating my family like this every day, but I did feel some level of stress almost every day from panic over my unsuccessful efforts and what I considered to be my unsuccessful life.

I'm guessing you can relate to my ongoing sense that I was hanging on by a thread, trying to survive life but never truly enjoying it. No wonder we're exhausted by the end of the day!

Believe it or not, this sense of failure isn't just a modern-day phenomenon. The apostle Paul described his disappointment with his own shortcomings:

> What I don't understand about myself is that I decide one way, but then I act another, doing things I absolutely despise. So if I can't be trusted to figure out what is best for myself and then do it, it becomes obvious that God's command is necessary.
>
> But I need something *more*! For if I know the law but still can't keep it, and if the power of sin within me keeps sabotaging my best intentions, I obviously need help! I realize that I don't have what it takes. I can will it, but I can't *do* it. I decide to do good, but I don't *really* do it; I decide not to do bad, but then I do it anyway. My decisions, such as they are, don't result in actions. Something has gone wrong deep within me and gets the better of me every time.
>
> It happens so regularly that it's predictable. The moment I decide

to do good, sin is there to trip me up. I truly delight in God's commands, but it's pretty obvious that not all of me joins in that delight. Parts of me covertly rebel, and just when I least expect it, they take charge.

I've tried everything and nothing helps. I'm at the end of my rope. Is there no one who can do anything for me? Isn't that the real question? (Romans 7:15–24, MSG)

None of us is a stranger to this internal struggle that Paul described. We've tried everything, just as he noted in verse 24, but no matter how strong our determination to do the right thing, somehow we keep sabotaging our own best intentions.

I lived here for so long. Whether it was a health problem, a character flaw, or the fact that I had failed yet again at checking off all the items on my list, falling short of my ideals just made me that much more determined to come up with a solution for the problem of me. I'd search the Internet for the answer to my current health crisis, immediately put my discoveries into action, and start telling everyone else about how I found this particular health solution that I was sure could also benefit them. I would read a passage in the Bible or listen to a sermon podcast hoping to get an answer for my current character flaw, then I would say to myself, *Okay, I've got the answer now! I'm going to be more like Jesus tomorrow.* Regarding the day-to-day demands of life, I would think, *I've got to get life right today. I can't keep falling short, so let me think . . . What new method do I need to put into place to be successful today?*

Just about the time I finally mastered one health regimen or organizational system, I'd realize it wasn't working like I hoped, so I would switch to something new in an attempt to get a better result. I was so stressed, tired, anxious—and did I mention frustrated? You can guess that my family felt pretty much the same.

It took many, many years, but eventually I came to the place that Paul did in verse 24. I came to the end of my rope. And that's where God showed me how to shift my focus from my flaws to His forgiveness.

VICTORY OVER SIN

The road to victory over sin is paved with right believing. The problem is that, even after salvation, many of us still wrongly believe ourselves to be sinners, rather than seeing ourselves as new creations in Christ, with new natures.

Let me explain. Along with all humanity, you and I were born into sin. In other words, we are sinners because of Adam, whose choice in the Garden of Eden introduced sin into the world for all of humanity (see Romans 5:12). That means everyone who has ever been born—and who will ever be born—is born into sin. That doesn't sound fair, does it? But keep reading, because this deal is about to turn to your advantage!

Our condition as sinners separated us from a holy God, who cannot look on evil (see Habakkuk 1:13). But God wanted so much to be in close relationship with us that He sent His perfect Son into the world to die on the cross for us, to serve as the one final sacrifice that would forever cover our sins. "For God made Christ, who never sinned, to be the offering for our sin, so that we could be made right with God through Christ" (2 Corinthians 5:21). At the cross all that we deserved fell on Jesus and all that Jesus deserved fell on us! While it may not have seemed fair that we were all born into sin because of Adam, neither does it seem fair that Jesus took everything we deserved—all the consequences of our sin, past, present, and future—upon Himself in an agonizing death.

> At the cross all that we deserved fell on Jesus and all that Jesus deserved fell on us!

But that's exactly how God chose to make everything right:

If death got the upper hand through one man's wrongdoing, can you imagine the breathtaking recovery life makes, sovereign life, in those who grasp with both hands this wildly extravagant life-gift, this grand setting-everything-right, that the one man Jesus Christ provides? (Romans 5:17, MSG)

This verse is so good I want to quote it in another translation too:

For the sin of this one man, Adam, caused death to rule over many. But even greater is God's wonderful grace and his gift of righteousness, for all who receive it will live in triumph over sin and death through this one man, Jesus Christ. (Romans 5:17)

Because of one Man's act of obedience, because of Jesus' finished work on the cross, all those who believe in and accept Christ have been given a gift of righteousness, a gift of right standing with God.

For years I totally missed what this gift meant for me. I knew I was sinning and failing, failing and sinning, but I didn't understand why. Finally, watching Andy Stanley's DVD series *Free* helped me realize that, instead of viewing myself as a new creation in Christ with a new nature, I still saw myself as the same person I was before salvation—a sinner. (You can access Andy Stanley's wonderful teaching series online for free at http://wecan befree.org.)

Before salvation, each of us is a sinner (noun) at the very core of our being, which causes us to sin (verb). But once we receive Jesus as our Savior, we are taken out of Adam and placed in Christ. Who we are, at the very core of our being, has changed.

In Romans, Paul explains that our new identity—who we are in Christ—affects more than just our eternal destination. It's not as if we're left to somehow muddle through life on this earth while we await the promise of heaven. No, when we receive Jesus, we are thoroughly changed in the here and now. You are no longer a sinner. I am no longer a sinner. Instead, we have "become the righteousness of God in Him [Christ]" (2 Corinthians 5:21, NKJV).

This doesn't mean that we never sin, but that *being a sinner* is no longer our identity. Instead, *being the righteousness of God in Christ* is our identity! Notice I did not use the phrase *being righteous;* this change is not about any good works we do or because of our righteous deeds. I am talking about *the righteousness of God* as a noun, as our new identity because of Jesus. Just as sin was the outgrowth of what was once true of us at the core, now that we have received Jesus, righteousness is an outgrowth of what is now true of us at the core.

We have the privilege of living our lives through Christ! We didn't do anything to earn this privilege. It was given to us 100 percent free!

Understanding and believing this is a big, big deal because, as we noted earlier, right believing always leads to right living. If we believe we are still sinners, then we will keep sinning. But if we believe we have been made righteous, then good fruit will be produced in our lives by the power of the Holy Spirit.

So when we are tempted to sin, the very best thing we can believe and say right in the middle of that temptation is "I am the righteousness of God in Christ." (Or, as we taught our twin girls to say, "I'm a good girl in Jesus!") It reminds us of who we really are and that sin is no longer our master and does not have dominion over us.

Reminding ourselves who we are in Christ certainly affects our approach to temptation in a positive way. I have been in Christ since I was eight years old, but for much of my life I chose to live by my own rules, trying to get free from sin by my own methods. Of course, trying harder to get free was point-less because my old self, the one born in Adam (the one I was still identifying with), would never be capable of overcoming temptation. Had I spent all that energy instead on growing in my relationship with Jesus, on studying the wonderful promises in the Bible, and on remembering who the new-and-improved me in Christ really was, I would have saved myself a truckload of anxiety and frustration.

FROM HARD LABOR TO EFFORTLESS CHANGE

I love what my friend Cally once wrote to me: "The enemy would love to get us to 'work' our will into submission (since it cannot be done) rather than receive the submission and permanent changes that come as a result of grace."

I truly believe God changes us effortlessly, through the power of His Spirit, on the other side of grace. The word *effortlessly* used to worry me, and I've heard a lot of other people express the same concern, so I want to explain what I mean. I feel this deserves clarification because I really want to see Christians begin to live from a place of resting in Christ instead of from a place of struggle, struggle, struggle. Now that I've seen for myself the differ-ence it makes to live under grace, I know without a doubt that it's not God's will for us to struggle all the time. A life of rest is what God wants for every one of His children. Rest is our spiritual promised land!

There is a big difference between living by our own efforts and living in response to the leading of the Spirit. Self-effort is when we try to get the job—any job—done in our own strength. This applies to a job such as de-veloping spiritual maturity, and it applies to tangible tasks, like the job I'm doing right now in editing this book. For both situations, what I have to say fits the bill: doing anything by our self-effort will make it feel like hard labor, the kind that causes us to be anxious and frustrated on the inside.

As my husband, Steve, says, "Living in frustration is the opposite of living in grace." Self-effort is the same thing as works. Remember how we earlier read Paul's declaration in Romans 11:6 that if something is of grace, then it's not of works, and if it's of works, then it's not of grace? Grace leaves no room for man's works. But once we come under grace—when we surrender, submit, yield, receive grace through faith—in any area of life, we will find the Holy Spirit leading us, guiding us, giving us wisdom, and showing us steps to handle whatever we face. Then we can simply respond to the Spirit's lead. Can I tell you the best news? When God's grace comes on the scene,

> A life of rest is what God wants for every one of His children. Rest is our spiritual promised land!

it produces in us a heart change, giving us the desire to obey, the desire to walk in wisdom, and the desire to follow the Spirit. I am telling you, it really is a completely different kind of existence. Those willing to lay down their self-efforts and to go the way of grace will discover that grace changes them, effortlessly, from the inside out!

Yes, I work deliberately toward each goal in life, but when I do it by the grace of God, I experience a flow and peace so that the work doesn't feel like hard labor. The apostle Paul explains this so brilliantly: "But whatever I am now, it is all because God poured out his special favor on me—and not without results. For I have worked harder than any of the other apostles; yet it was not I but God who was working through me by his grace" (1 Corinthians 15:10).

So when I say *effortlessly,* I mean that once we have chosen to live under grace (which is really a decision we make moment by moment), we will have the "want to" to do the things God wants because of the change His grace has made in our hearts; therefore, we will be able to respond to the Spirit's lead effortlessly. In fact, Jesus is more than willing to live His life through us once we choose to surrender to Him. As the apostle Paul said, "It was not I but God who was working through me by his grace."

The key is to receive God's grace on a continual basis. As I'm working on my second round of edits for this book, at times my brain starts to feel fried. That's exactly when I have a decision to make. Am I going to kick into high gear with my own effort, through gritted teeth, saying, *I can do this. Let me just exert more willpower.* Or will this be my cue to pray, *Dear God, I come to You in the name of Jesus, and I choose to receive more of Your grace right now to finish these edits*? Maybe that comes through listening to a couple of worship songs or by just taking a break and hanging out with my kids. God will always show us how we can become refreshed if we turn to Him.

As we learn to rely continually on grace, a task that used to feel like hard labor suddenly becomes smooth sailing. This is exactly why I get so much more accomplished from an attitude of rest and peace than I used to accomplish with anxiety and frustration. My former, unproductive, ineffective life was lived almost solely by Sandra's efforts. Yes, I might have sprinkled in just a little bit of grace once in a while, but that doesn't work either. Grace and self-effort do not mix.

No wonder Paul basically asked the Galatians if they had lost their minds, since they had entered into the restful life of grace, then decided to return to their former life of legalism. Paul said, "Something crazy has happened" (3:1, MSG).

My friend, the only work you have to do in order to enter into this wonderful, new, grace-filled life is to believe (see John 6:29). You do not have to produce all kinds of good fruit to earn your way into God's grace. The truth is exactly the opposite: your humble acceptance of God's great grace (undeserved favor) will send you on a fruit-bearing venture the likes of nothing you've ever seen before in your life. In his teaching series *Free,* Andy Stanley paraphrases Jesus' encouragement to His followers to abide in Him: "If you'll learn the secret, if you'll change your mind-set, if you'll just change your entire approach to following Me so that it's no longer rule keeping and law failing and become abiding and remaining, here's what's gonna happen: you're gonna look behind you, and there's gonna be fruit, and people are gonna say, 'You've changed.' And you're gonna say, 'I know, but I'm not really sure how.' . . . 'I feel—I feel like I'm doing less than I've ever done.'" Andy explains that this happens simply "because you're learning to abide. And you'll look over your shoulder, and there will be fruit, more fruit."[3] Or as Jesus said, "When you produce much fruit, you are my true disciples" (John 15:8). This way of life draws everyone's eyes toward Jesus—which is exactly as it should be!

Instead of thinking of grace as an abstract concept or idea, as a subject or as one message, think of Jesus, and when you think of Jesus, think of grace, for Jesus is God's grace personified! (See Romans 5:15; and Ephesians 2:8, NASB; Titus 2:11; Titus 3:4–6, AMP.) I like to say, just get to grace and grace will take you from there, or with this in mind, just get to Jesus and Jesus will take you from there!

WHEN WE CHOOSE GRIT OVER GRACE

Grace is our escape from temptation, the strength to live fully in our new identity of righteousness in Christ. In Galatians 5:16 Paul wrote, "So I tell you, live the way the Spirit leads you. Then you will not do the evil things your sinful self wants" (ERV). But sometimes we choose not to follow the lead of the Holy Spirit and instead try to grit it out on our own, approaching temptation as if we can conquer it through pure determination. When we fail—and we will—God's grace remains ready to catch us. This has proven true in my life, time and again.

Not long ago my daughter Angel received a knitting machine for Christmas. I don't know one thing about knitting, so on Christmas Day I spent a decent amount of time reading the directions to figure out how to help Angel use her new present. (I had mistakenly thought we were done with assembling presents once we got past the dollhouse stage!) When I finally understood how to work the machine, we started in—only to find out that the yarn supplied with the machine seemed to be pretty tangled up. I said, "Let's work on this yarn tomorrow, then we can try again."

The next morning I started unwinding the ball of yarn, eager for Angel to be able to use her new present. I kept thinking, *Once I get this next knot out, it should open up,* but it never did. I truly have never seen so many knots in my life.

At about the two-hour mark, my initial peace started turning into frustration. I should note that I've learned that frustration is nearly always a signal that I am not resting in God's grace. But I totally ignored the blaring alarm and pressed ahead. Steve, my husband, suggested we throw away that yarn and go to the local craft store to buy a new skein. I appreciated the suggestion, but I wouldn't hear of it. One of the things I most despise in life is wasted, unproductive time. The only way in my mind to justify the two hours I'd already invested was to push through until I succeeded in untangling the knots.

This is the point at which I chose not to live under the grace of God and instead allowed my self-efforts to kick into high gear.

I soon had the girls helping me unwind the yarn, which, despite their good attitudes, was not how they wanted to spend their Christmas vacation. But I was determined to succeed on my self-appointed mission. As we continued working for several more hours, I declared, "I don't care if I have to stay up until midnight to get this accomplished. I never give up." Notice how many times I used the word *I.* That's a clear sign that I was not receiving

God's grace. By now I absolutely knew that I was operating in the flesh instead of in the power of the Holy Spirit, but my fear of failure compelled me onward. I just knew I was getting closer to success.

This is when my daughter Angel started dancing to the music we had playing. Unaware that the yarn was wrapped around her, she spun in circles. As I set to work on this whole new set of knots she'd created, I made it abundantly clear to Angel that I didn't appreciate the additional work. I know, I know—it's not like she did it on purpose. She was just being a kid, having fun.

The problem was not Angel or the tangled skein of yarn or even the company that shipped it that way, though you wouldn't have found me saying so at the time! The problem was that I was totally ignoring the Holy Spirit, and I knew it. Instead of submitting to the grace of God to help me out of this flesh fit, I listened to the devil's suggestion that I point fingers and place blame instead of facing my own bad choice.

The thought of giving up on my yarn-unwinding mission sent my thoughts and emotions into panic mode. If I quit, that would mean I was a failure. In retrospect it seems silly that I would have tied my worth to a pile of yarn, but I believe we all make similarly illogical choices at times. Often the way we react has roots in a specific incident in our past. In this case, my irrational response was probably rooted in the fact that I have never felt successful when it comes to arts and crafts. While I earned As and Bs in my other subjects, I barely made a C in art. I remember feeling bad about how my best efforts never seemed good enough. That sense of inadequacy followed me into adulthood. I just don't seem to have the gift for handcrafts that comes so naturally to many other women.

As I persisted in my efforts to untangle the yarn, I eventually blew up, angry at myself for making a stupid decision that ruined my plans for the day—plans that included some writing time for this book. Because I followed my flesh I lost a whole day of writing.

Thankfully, our God is a God who redeems our mistakes. I'm sharing this story in the certainty that He will use my willfulness to encourage others—and remind me!—to choose to live under the ease of God's grace instead of forcing things to happen the way we think they are supposed to. The great news is that even when we do make the wrong choice, we do not have to beat ourselves up over it. In fact, the only way to truly get free from our weakness is by welcoming His grace.

> But He said to me, My grace (My favor and loving-kindness and mercy) is enough for you [sufficient against any danger and enables you to bear the trouble manfully]; for My strength and power are made perfect (fulfilled and completed) and show themselves most effective in [your] weakness. Therefore, I will all the more gladly glory in my weaknesses and infirmities, that the strength and power of Christ (the Messiah) may rest (yes, may pitch a tent over and dwell) upon me! (2 Corinthians 12:9, AMP)

After losing my temper, I eventually calmed down and had this conversation with God: *God, I am so sorry that I didn't listen to You when the peace was gone. I know that's my signal to stop and switch gears, and I just totally ignored it. I thank You so much that I am already forgiven since Jesus paid the price for my sin on the cross. I receive Your forgiveness. I don't receive guilt since that would be me trying to pay for my bad choices today and dishonoring Jesus' finished work. I thank You that I am the righteousness of God in Christ Jesus and You love me so much. Holy Spirit, I know You are helping me make the right choices in the future so I won't lose one moment of sleep over this. It's forgiven and forgotten according to Your wonderful promise in Hebrews 8:12.*

This was not an easy prayer for me. My inclination was to feel I didn't deserve His grace and to believe that I should continue to feel horrible for the atmosphere of tension I had created in my home. But wallowing in guilt and condemnation would have put me right back in the swamp of self-effort, trying to work up sufficient guilt and repentance to "deserve" forgiveness. I wanted to place my trust in Jesus' finished work, so I received God's mercy and forgiveness. Yes, I could have received His grace hours earlier and spared myself the embarrassment in front of my family, but that was a lesson learned for the next time.

Steve had taken the girls out to get ice cream, but when they returned, I sincerely apologized and asked for their forgiveness. They were so merciful, as always.

Trying to control life is completely exhausting, so I was emotionally and physically wiped out after all this was over. Like many people, I tend to turn to comfort foods, specifically desserts, when I've had a stressful day. This really is not good for my waistline or my health, so this time instead of dipping my spoon into some cookie-dough ice cream, I plugged in my iPod and listened to my "God Loves Me" playlist—a library of songs all about God's great love for me. When I started listening, the presence of the Lord comforted me far beyond any comfort ice cream could ever have provided. I immediately began to relax.

> Wallowing in guilt and condemnation would have put me right back in the swamp of self-effort, trying to work up sufficient guilt and repentance to "deserve" forgiveness.

It felt good to remember that, no matter how many times I blow it, God's love isn't going anywhere.

5

Are You Ready to Let God Love You?

The Grace-Led Life Frees Us from the Weight of Guilt

As we've discussed, sometimes the reason we are not seeing the change we desire is because we are trying to bring about the change by the strength of our flesh. We think to ourselves, *I just need to love God more to get free from this sin. If I loved God enough, I would try harder and get free from this struggle.* But I would propose that change comes when we let God love us right in the middle of our failures, when we allow God to pour His grace on our wounds, and when we completely receive the gift of righteousness that God has given us apart from our works. In these unmerited gifts, in this unmerited favor, we gain His strength to overcome temptation and sin.

Today I was late once again. (Sigh.) Punctuality has been my lifelong struggle. Just ask anyone who knows me. I was tempted to be mad at myself for being late, but I thought, *Nope, that was the old Sandra. The new Sandra doesn't operate like that anymore.* Now I have something that I didn't know I had before: I have the gift of righteousness (see Romans 3:24).

See, the Lord told me years ago that if I would get ready first when I had somewhere I needed to be, I would always be on time. But I liked doing what I wanted to do more than what the Lord instructed me to do. I wanted to get my e-mails cleared out, clean and organize my house, and get all the details of my list checked off so I could get more check marks before leaving. Remember, the more items I checked off my daily task list, the more valuable I felt.

As a result of my fear, I was not giving Jesus lordship in this area of my life. Instead, I tried to figure out a way to free myself from the habit of being late. I tried so many different things, and once in a while I would discover a time-management method that I thought was my answer and immediately put it into action. But I was not depending on God's grace to help me—not one bit. I would pray, but then I would go right back to my self-efforts.

Come to find out, the very strength I needed to get past being late and start being on time was *not* found in my trying desperately to stop being late or in being angry at myself when I failed, but rather it was found in my receiving God's love, forgiveness, and gift of righteousness right in the middle of being late.

Did you see that? Trying to get free and getting mad every time I failed was not the solution, but actually perpetuated my problem. The fact that God loves me just as much when I make a mistake is hard to wrap my head around, but that is what makes grace . . . grace. And some months ago, this truth is exactly what I started putting into practice each time I found myself running late.

Instead of receiving the guilt and condemnation that Satan wanted to bury me under, I reminded myself of the truth, saying out loud in my car over and over again: "I am the righteousness of God in Christ. I am not less righteous now because I am late. His gift of righteousness is not based on my works. His gift of righteousness to me is solely based on what Jesus did for me on the cross. I am not more righteous on days I live more perfectly and less righteous on days I live less perfectly, because my righteousness is 'in Christ,' not in myself. God loves me right now, right in the middle of being late."

I didn't deceive myself about my problem. I acknowledged that being late is inconsiderate to the person waiting on me and to my family as I stress them out trying to rush out the door. But I reminded myself that this doesn't change God's view of me. "God loves me," I declared aloud. "He doesn't love me less right now. He is love, and therefore, He never stops loving me.

> The fact that God loves me just as much when I make a mistake is hard to wrap my head around, but that is what makes grace ... grace.

He is with me, right now, and He will never leave me." Of course, as I recalled God's goodness toward me, repentance was also on my lips because God's goodness leads us to repentance (see Romans 2:4, NKJV).

I deliberately took this approach several times while rushing to get somewhere, knowing I was going to arrive late. To my surprise, I began to notice a shift in my attitude. After about three times of intentionally remembering—in the midst of being late—God's unconditional love toward me, His complete forgiveness of me, and my righteousness in Him apart from my works, I told my husband, "Something has changed in my thinking. I have this new desire to walk in love with people—both the person who is waiting to meet me, by being on time, and my family, you and the girls, by not rushing around causing stress in your lives." I mention three times not as some magic number but to point out how fast grace brought change in this area that I had struggled with my whole life. I mean I even remember regularly chasing the elementary-school bus down our street because I would leave my house too late to get to the bus stop on time. So I'm not kidding when I say this had been a longstanding problem.

My own efforts, my own discipline, my own strength, and my own way were simply no match for the grace of God. Right believing about God's love for me, my righteousness in Him, and my complete forgiveness through Jesus' blood paved the way to right living. The Lord now has my will in this area, the very will I tried to beat into submission for years. I no longer go around thinking, *I have to start being on time. I must get over this hang-up. I'm such a sinner.* Now what comes to my mind is, *I want to walk in love with these people. I want to obey God.*

You see, we can never find lasting change in any area of our lives, including character development, apart from the grace of God. As I'm sure you too have experienced, trying to force change from the outside in is frustrating and ineffective. By contrast, grace transforms us from the inside out. This is why I suddenly began to desire to walk in greater love toward people with regard to being on time! Thank You, Holy Spirit!

After enjoying freedom in this area for quite a while, I again began to arrive late almost everywhere I went. Anxiety crept into my thinking: *I've got to get a handle on this again. I have to stop sinning in this area. I have to obey God.* But soon the Holy Spirit reminded me to turn to right believing. I chose to remember that I am unconditionally loved by God, righteous in Christ apart from my works, and completely forgiven because of the blood of Jesus. Shortly after I refocused on right believing, I began to walk in love with people again by being on time far more often!

Do you see here how I had to intentionally receive God's unmerited favor (grace) right in the middle of my failure? When I did, the Holy Spirit went to work, changing me from the inside out. When I stopped working, He started working!

This reminds me of a lady in our small-group Bible study at church, who described for us how God's grace impacted her during an argument with her husband. "Right in the middle of our fight," she said, "God showed me to go ahead and receive His grace." She told us she was in shock at first because, in her mind, she couldn't receive grace until she had made everything right with her husband—until she got her mess cleaned up. But in reality Jesus, who is Grace, stepped in and cleaned up her mess as soon as she chose to put her faith in Him.

And God will do the same for you and me every time we choose to receive His gift of grace right in the middle of our failures.

WHAT ABOUT REPENTANCE?

Someone e-mailed me recently to ask whether or not we need to repent since we're living under grace. What a great question! I can tell you that the answer has had a significant impact on my entire family.

As I mentioned already, Romans 2:4 says that the goodness of God leads us to repentance. I have certainly found this to be true. Under grace, repenting is a consistent part of my lifestyle; however, the nature of my repentance is entirely different from how I used to approach it. For instance, if I read the Bible and see something that doesn't match my life, I now think, *Yes, Lord, I change my mind about that. I choose to think differently now—according to Your Word.* That's repentance! The Greek word translated as "repentance" is *metanoia,* and it literally means "a change of mind."

This is a huge shift from all the years when Steve and I thought we had to repent in order to obtain God's forgiveness. This wrong believing caused us to constantly feel like we were in God's good graces, then out of God's good graces, in and then out again, based on our behavior and on how quickly we repented. We were never secure in our relationship with God because we behaved as if it were based on our own works. We did not understand that as believers in Jesus we were (and are) already completely forgiven for all our sins—past, present, and future (see Colossians 2:13–14 and Hebrews 10:11–12)! I can't tell you how good it felt to finally understand that, because of Jesus, we are in God's good graces—permanently and forever!

When we finally grasped the truth of God's grace, we realized we had been disregarding and dishonoring what Jesus had done for us on the cross when He shed His blood for our sins. I know this sounds terrible, but before I understood grace, who I am in Christ, and the New Covenant, I rarely ever thought about what Jesus did for me on the cross or what He provided for me through His finished work. I was too busy counting up all my sins all the time and forever trying to figure out ways to be a "good Christian." I was extremely self-conscious and sin-conscious.

The revelation that we are totally forgiven didn't make Steve and me stop repenting, but it did make us stop being sin-conscious (see Hebrews 10:1–22). Our repentance was no longer accompanied by fear, guilt, or the thought that *if I do this just right and make sure I repent often enough, then I will earn forgiveness.* Instead, we find ourselves thinking, *You've got to be kidding, God! You mean to tell me that I am completely forgiven forever?*

I guarantee you that any person who is truly living under God's grace will be repenting on a regular basis. It just becomes part of your lifestyle because you fall so deeply in love with Jesus from understanding and dwelling on everything He has done for you! You are constantly seeing God's goodness, and as a result you are constantly making adjustments, changing your mind, and choosing to go in a different direction!

So how do we approach repentance in specific ways now that we are living under grace? Here's a personal example. Let's say I speak to my twin girls in a less-than-desirable manner. Before I fully understood grace, I would apologize to my girls and ask them to forgive me (which was good), but then I would immediately feel guilt ridden and condemned. I believed that God was displeased with me and that I would have to stand outside His presence until I repented and *got myself* back into His good graces again. Anxious and fearful, I would immediately go into self-effort mode, trying to think of a way to be sure I would never make that mistake again.

Now that I'm living under grace, when I realize I've been impatient, I still apologize to my girls and ask them to forgive me—but then I go right into thanking God for and receiving the forgiveness already provided for me because of what my wonderful Savior did on the cross!

In my new way of responding to sin, under grace, I don't get caught up in worry or self-condemnation about the fact that I just sinned. Instead, I immediately turn to Jesus and center my thoughts on how good He is to me—how He forgives me and never again remembers my sins (see Hebrews 8:12).

Time after time after time, as I look away from my less-than-perfect self and look to my perfect Savior, I truly begin to change my mind—to repent. I realize that I totally want to speak to my girls in a respectful and honoring tone. Just as the scripture says, God's goodness leads us to repentance.

And as I center my heart not on my sin or failure but on Jesus in all His beauty and perfection, His grace, which I received through right believing, produces in me the power I need to follow through. I move forward with confidence, knowing that the grace of God is at work within me to strengthen me in my area of weakness. Man, I get so excited in my spirit when I talk about this!

So yes, Steve and I believe in repentance—not as a means to get forgiveness but as a response to the goodness of God, as an acknowledgment of having already received His forgiveness. It's just our natural response to God's goodness for everything He has done for us!

We feel so sad when we see people who spend the majority of their time focusing on and talking about their failures. We used to do this too, and we vividly recall how that consistently led us back into lives of guilt, fear, and self-effort. But thankfully, because of the amazing grace of God, Steve and I and our children have discovered the phenomenal difference that comes with being conscious of what Jesus did right rather than what we do wrong. All four of us are walking in a level of peace beyond anything that we have ever enjoyed before!

REST IN YOUR RIGHTEOUS IDENTITY

When we gain freedom in an area through right believing, we need to realize we can lose that freedom if we stop relying on the grace of God. But the great news is, God's grace will always be present for us to tap into once again. All we have to do is make the choice to accept it and live in it!

We have to keep reminding ourselves of this truth: my identity is no longer sinner but righteous. My identity is in Christ.[4] We can declare this in any number of ways. Here are a few statements I've found to be personally helpful:

- I am the righteousness of God in Christ (see 2 Corinthians 5:21).
- Sin is not my master (see Romans 6:14).
- Sin holds no power over me (see Romans 6:7).
- I am dead to sin but alive to God in Christ Jesus (see Romans 6:11).
- *For kids:* I am a good girl or good boy *in Jesus.*

Believe the truth of your identity and declare it with confidence—when you're having a good day, when you're being tempted, when you're on your way to sinning, right in the middle of sinning, and even after sinning—until your thinking becomes unshakably grounded in the reality of who you are in Christ.

For you to experience the power of your new life in Christ, you can't just believe this once, then after you sin, say, "Oh well, that didn't work." No, if you consistently believe that you are the righteousness of God in Christ and speak it, you *will* experience a change and see an explosion of spiritual fruit in your life. Guilt and condemnation will not change you or me; we are transformed by receiving and believing in the righteousness that Jesus died to give us!

My friend Helene describes so beautifully the change that came when the truth of God's grace opened up for her. Though she and her husband trusted the Lord to lead and guide them when they began their ministry, somewhere along the way she began putting more faith in her performance than in Jesus. "I wondered if I was obedient enough," she told me. "I asked myself, *Am I praying enough? Did I read my Bible enough today?* My eyes were no longer fixed on my wonderful Savior and Redeemer but on my performance."

Does any of this sound as familiar to you as it does to me? Thank God He didn't leave Helene to struggle alone.

She prayed daily the words of Paul in Philippians 3:10 (NKJV): "that I may know Him and the power of His resurrection," along with Ephesians 1:18, asking that the eyes of her understanding would be enlightened to all that Christ had done for her. With joy, she told me, "He does watch over His Word to perform it, He brings the light of His glorious gospel into the deepest condemned area, and He allows just enough light to shine in so that we hunger for that freedom, that love, that release of all the burdens we place upon ourselves."

In answer to Helene's prayers, the Spirit of God began to light up His Word for her in a new and glorious way. "Everything I read seemed to have a clearer meaning," she said. "Everything I read pointed to what Jesus had already done and had already made available for those who believe. *Only believe!* It jumped out at me. *Only believe!* not *Only do!*"

Her early passion for God returned, more alive, more enlightened, and definitely with a greater understanding of His grace. "Only now," she said, "it isn't about my loving Him, but about how much He loves me! It's not about what I do for Him, but what He did for me!"

She has discovered the glorious freedom that comes when we rest in the finished work of Christ. "No longer do I walk in the guilt and condemnation and fear of not doing enough to walk in the straight and narrow path," Helene explained. "His love surrounds me and keeps me in His path, just like those guardrails they put along the bowling lane for little children so their bowling balls don't go in the gutter but hit the pins every time. What security, what joy, what peace. Fear has been removed, and now I spend each day resting in His love for me."

Helene's story makes me so glad that we do not have to be sin-conscious but can instead be Christ-conscious. We are richly blessed to be welcomed into the New Covenant. Jesus is completely amazing! The book of Ephesians describes for us the power that comes from comprehending the depths of God's love and letting it enfold us:

> And I ask him that with both feet planted firmly on love, you'll be
> able to take in with all followers of Jesus the extravagant dimensions
> of Christ's love. Reach out and experience the breadth! Test its length!
> Plumb the depths! Rise to the heights! Live full lives, full in the
> fullness of God. (3:17–19, MSG)

I love these verses!

Choosing to personally receive and rest in God's extravagant love is one of the wisest things we can do. It frees us from condemnation and produces the divine empowerment we need to live in victory over sin. When we regularly drink deeply of God's love and let it fill us up, we don't have room for anxiety or frustration. When our hearts are overflowing with God's grace, we no longer view ourselves as sinners but as children of the King.

We looked earlier at Romans 5:17, but let's look at this healing truth once more, in the Amplified Bible:

> For if because of one man's trespass (lapse, offense) death reigned through that one, much more surely will those who receive [God's] overflowing grace (unmerited favor) and the free gift of righteousness [putting them into right standing with Himself] reign as kings in life through the one Man Jesus Christ (the Messiah, the Anointed One).

We can "reign as kings in life." What a promise! And all because Jesus Christ has overcome all our flaws and failures!

You can apply this to any area you are struggling in. Remind yourself that when you became a Christian, you were given a gift of righteousness—a gift that was not based on your performance. Remind yourself that you have a new nature because when Jesus died on the cross, you died with Him, and when He was raised from the dead, the new and improved you was raised with Him. One of the qualities of your new nature is the desire to walk in love and to experience God's power at work within you. When you see yourself as new, you will not desire to remain in sin, but you will instead want to live in the promises that are included in the New Covenant. Right believing leads to right living!

A friend told me recently that someone said to her, "You people just say you live in grace so you can do whatever you want." My immediate response to her was, "Oh no, that's not grace at all." Then the two of us talked about how the grace we believe in is God's unmerited favor, producing Jesus' power within us and changing us from the inside out as we receive it, even in the midst of our failures. My friend and I gave each other high-fives because we know firsthand what a growing understanding of grace has done in our own lives, and at the same time we also completely realize it is only through Jesus' life in us that these things have been accomplished!

When we understand and choose to live under grace, we won't, of course, be perfect, but there will be a noticeable and progressive transformation in our lives as we continue to put our faith in, and live surrendered to, the power of Christ within us. In fact, under these circumstances it would be impossible for us *not* to experience a remarkable transformation. True grace is in Christ, by Christ, and through Christ alone!

Grace doesn't give you a license to sin. Grace gives you the strength to look away from your old self and your own way of trying to be and do right—and instead look to Christ in you, what He has done and who you are in Him.

Pastor and author Joseph Prince explains how this certainty equips us to be overcomers, no matter what the devil throws our way:

> The power of Jesus to overcome every temptation kicks in when you remain conscious that even at the point of temptation, Jesus is **still** with you and that you are righteous in Him apart from your works! When you do that, you reject the condemnation for the temptation that you faced. You now have the power of Christ to rise above your temptation and to rest in your righteous identity in Christ apart from your works. That, beloved, is the overcoming life in Christ![5]

You want more confidence? Put all of your trust in the finished work of the Cross and none in your own works. Your confidence will soar, because Jesus' finished work is perfect and never fails in any way! I have seen this happen with myself and the rest of my family. We are so much more confident now because our assurance isn't based on ourselves but on our righteous identity in Jesus. Jesus is always with us and will never leave us, confident in good times or in bad.

ROOTED IN HIS LOVE

God loves us with a love beyond what any human can offer. His love literally makes us whole. I am now like a little kid in knowing that God loves me. In years past I couldn't stop obsessing over the things I always did wrong and feeling bad about them, but now I really have a sense of being God's daughter. I like to call myself God's girl!

In the previous chapter I described a time I failed to submit to God's grace while unwinding yarn. Now I'd like to share one of my experiences in submitting to grace rather than depending on self-effort.

Recently, I needed to forgive someone. Initially I went into anxiety mode, thinking, *I'm so upset but I can't feel this way. I have to forgive. I need to watch my thinking.* Thankfully, this train of thought lasted only about ten seconds before I prayed, *Dear God, I place myself under Your grace. Thank You for helping me forgive.* The next thing I started thinking about was how I also have done the very same thing as the person I was mad at. I meditated on how much Jesus has forgiven me of (getting back to right believing). After about five minutes of this, I felt a release in my heart because I suddenly had the desire to forgive this person. God's grace changed my "I have to," "I'd better," and "I need to" into "I want to." I forgave the person right then. It was over that easily. I have not had one bad thought about that individual since. Thank God for His grace.

If I was still anxiously trying to figure out what I could do in my self-efforts to be able to forgive, I would still be trying to forgive that person. God's will is not for us to fight, but to rest and rely on His grace. He wants us to stop trying to figure out a way in our own strength to get free, to turn to Him, to receive the power that comes from meditating on and living in His unmerited favor, to follow the leading of the Spirit, to come out victorious on the other side of grace—and then to move on so we can be used to advance His kingdom!

Victory does not come through beating ourselves up every time we make a mistake. If we get free by our own efforts, we'll be inclined to boast in ourselves and in our methods. But when we experience victory by looking to Him, we know that only by God's grace are we free from that sin that entangled us for so long. Knowing this will propel us to be thankful and boast only in Him! We'll find ourselves constantly pointing people to Jesus, because we want Him to get all the glory. "But in all these things we overwhelmingly conquer through Him who loved us" (Romans 8:37, NASB).

Many Christians don't know how much God loves them. They need that assurance—they need to see His love at work in our lives. They have many misconceptions about Him, sometimes including a belief that He is mad at them. I believe these misconceptions keep Christians from drawing close to God; instead of reveling in His grace, they live anxiously under the burdens of legalism and perfectionism. I also fully believe that as more Christians grasp true grace, they will begin naturally sharing that grace with the world, which will lead more people to Jesus.

> Victory does not come through beating ourselves up every time we make a mistake.

The Gospels make it clear that imperfect people loved to hang around Jesus. They knew He genuinely cared about them. They didn't feel measured by Jesus; they felt loved by Him. He didn't look to see if they were following the rules before inviting Himself into their world because He knew that His entrance into their world would transform them. The Pharisees, on the other hand, were more concerned with the rules than with the people themselves. They dragged the woman caught in adultery to Jesus in hopes that He would condemn her. Instead, He offered her His personal love and acceptance, and only after freely giving her these things did He tell her to go and sin no more (see John 8:1–11). You see, Jesus knew a secret that the Pharisees just didn't get: Jesus knew that extending His grace to that dear woman was the very thing that would give her the power to end her lifestyle of sin.

We are blessed to be living under the New Covenant, and it is such a tragedy that so many do not receive what Jesus died to provide for them. In my own experience—and I'm sure mine is like many, many other Christians'—I just did not understand what I had in Christ. Although I knew much of the Christian terminology, such as "I'm in Christ, I'm the righteousness of God in Christ, I have a brand new nature in Christ," my own legalism blinded me for years from truly grasping the transformative power of these truths until I genuinely began to understand grace.

Grace is like a breath of fresh air, and receiving God's grace helps us lay down our worries and breathe easier. Why? Because Jesus knows everything about us and yet He accepts us 100 percent. He knew Peter was going to deny Him, yet He prayed for Peter. He knew Judas was going to betray Him, but He still treated Judas with kindness.

God's love for us is so unimaginable that we will spend the rest of our lives discovering the riches of this treasure. Picture a little girl who has just opened up a treasure chest and, with a huge smile on her face, is pulling out piece after piece of beautiful gemstones and jewels. This is how I feel now that I am living my life on the foundation of God's amazing grace. And since God is certainly no respecter of persons, this can be your experience too!

6

Nothing You Do Will Change His Love for You

The Grace-Led Life Releases Us from the Pressure to Perform

As we've seen, the good news of God's grace is where the good life starts, after we finally realize our self-efforts will always come up short and we are ready to stop trying. At last we come to the end of ourselves and announce to God our utter failure at trying to live the Christian life.

Of course, He has known all along that we couldn't pull it off on our own. He's just been waiting for the moment when we say, *Jesus, take over. Only You can make me what I ought to be by living through me.* We did this the day we got saved. We were saved by grace, and God intended that we would continue to live the Christian life by grace. But our self-efforts kicked in. Then we went on this crazy works trip, continually trying to accomplish more, go farther, and be more perfect.

For years, I thought my circumstances were causing the frustration and anxiety in my life. My list of daily tasks frustrated me the most—from keeping the house clean to making sure we had healthy food choices in the fridge, from homeschooling my girls to running errands. I made every effort to keep my circumstances under control so I could feel like a success at the end of the day. I was fine as long as everything stayed on my schedule, but as you know, often our plans take a hit. Sometimes the girls would have a particularly hard day with their schoolwork, and if I was already too frustrated with life to be much of a help, this caused anxiety in the girls and led to bad attitudes. Other times, unexpected things would throw me off course. I had unrealistic expectations and planned my schedule to the minute; therefore, anything extra seemed like a bother and brought on frustration.

As I understood more about grace, I realized that many of my so-called problems were really the results of a wrong mind-set, and my wrong mind-set was a result of wrong believing in many areas of my life. I learned that our circumstances do not have nearly the impact that our thoughts and attitudes do. Our lives can be altered by the transformation of our minds even if our circumstances remain the same. I am living proof of this because, as I have been sharing, I am now relaxed and living in rest, yet my circumstances are no different than before. I still have all the responsibilities of a wife, mother, sister, daughter, and homeschooling mom, and I still have a long list of things to accomplish each week.

But I've come to understand that the gospel is not about how much we do for God; it's all about what He did for us—and what He continues to do through us. Christianity is not about our trying to be like Jesus as much as it is letting Jesus live His life through us. The difference matters enormously, because one mind-set focuses on us—and the other focuses on Jesus.

When my eyes finally opened to the true beauty of the gospel of grace, my response was an unquenchable desire to live full force for Him—but in the power of His strength alone. So if you're feeling like I did, battle weary from trying to live the Christian life, please know that He is just waiting for you to give up and let Him take over. Be assured, He will lead you on the most amazing journey ever!

ALL OURS TO ENJOY

When I continually had my nose stuck in my to-do list—desperately trying to be worth something—I rarely paid attention to the beauty all around me. I seldom noticed the amazing things God created to bring variety and wonder to our world. But ever since God helped me stop racing with myself, I feel as if life has shifted into slow motion. I now notice the beauty of nature, and to my surprise, I just love watching animals outside our house.

We put birdseed out on our deck in open boxes, and the birds that come to eat from our feeders are all just so beautiful. We are blessed with a wide variety of visitors, my favorite being the doves. Of course, the squirrels scurry up the support beams and onto the deck to help themselves to the birdseed. Each squirrel wants a feeder box to himself, so if another one gets close to his box, he'll start chasing the intruder. These squirrels bound around our yard, playing games with each other. It's adorable. It seems they have just one speed—fast—which makes them even more entertaining to watch.

We have purposely glued the feeders to the deck railing so we can see the birds and squirrels from our hearth room, kitchen, and family room. I'm convinced that they all love me because I feed them! I can sit and watch them for the longest time. They're so amusing.

In addition to birds and squirrels, we have seen lots of deer, including a number of fawns, a bobcat, a turkey, a fox, bunny rabbits, and chipmunks. Recently we even found a snake in our driveway. Several people assured us that it was just a garter snake and was actually beneficial to have around. (Though when I posted a picture and comment about this on Instagram, someone replied, "Repeat after me: *There are no good snakes!*")

The woods surrounding us make for amazing scenery every season of the year here in Missouri, where I've lived all my life. But previously, I was too caught up in my list of rules for living to ever notice the beauty of God's creation. I'm so glad He transformed my vision.

We had been living in our current home just a short while before I began to come into my personal revelation of God's grace. Maybe, just maybe, this house, with the view—which is my favorite thing about it—was one of the things that helped me discover the amazing world out there beyond my list. Now when I raise the shades around the house every morning, I feel as if God is looking down and winking at me. I can almost hear Him saying, *I love you, Sandra. You're My daughter. You're My girl!*

Just as the beauty of creation stands ready to wow us regardless of how much or how little we accomplished today, God's love also is ours to enjoy. He doesn't withhold it until we have marked off enough items on our spiritual checklist to "earn" His love. Ephesians 2 explains,

> But God is so rich in mercy, and he loved us so much, that even though we were dead because of our sins, he gave us life when he raised Christ from the dead. (It is only by God's grace that you have been saved!) For he raised us from the dead along with Christ and seated us with him in the heavenly realms because we are united with Christ Jesus. (verses 4–6)

His love endures forever!

God loved us freely when we were dead in sin, and He didn't switch us over to an earn-His-love program once we got saved. He won't love us any more if we succeed or any less if we fail. Whether we lead millions to Christ or no one at all, He will love us just the same.

Now, be honest—did that statement about leading people to Christ trigger the "I don't compute" switch in your brain? It sets mine off! I am still learning not to rate how much I think God loves a person, including me, based on what we do for Him. The fact that I had a hard time with that sentence proves that I have not yet fully grasped the breadth, length, height, and depth of His love for us—and that is okay (see Romans 8:38–39, NIV).

You and I get to continue unpacking God's great love over the entire span of our lifetimes. Isn't that great news?

Now, am I saying we shouldn't tell people about Jesus? Not at all! But no worries, because once you grasp God's grace, you will naturally be more of a witness for Christ than you ever were by your own efforts. That's really one

> God loved us freely when we were dead in sin, and He didn't switch us over to an earn-His-love program once we got saved.

of the main points of this book. All the things I was doing when I was living under the law and trying to please God through my own works—loving, giving, serving, witnessing, reading the Bible, praying—I still do, but no longer because of legalistic pressure. Rather, I do these things as a natural response to the amazing grace of my heavenly Father. Always remember that living under grace will take you light-years beyond any place that living under the law could ever take you.

THE AWESOME SIMPLICITY OF GRACE

When I learned that God delights in me simply because I am His daughter, *wow!* did that change everything for me. My mind was thrown into a tizzy. I was afraid that somehow I would be doing something wrong if I believed in the simplicity of grace. But I noticed something interesting in the midst of my growing revelation about God's grace: every time I came back to grace, my spirit would absolutely do backflips. Why?

Depending on my own efforts to keep all the rules perfectly always kept my eyes on myself and my own ability or, more often, my lack of ability. This resulted in almost continual anxiety and frustration. When I started depending on God's grace—everything He had already done for me—I started both relaxing and becoming majorly excited about my relationship with Jesus. In fact, I felt like I was being born again . . . all over again.

Wait a minute, Sandra, you might be thinking. *I thought you said you were afraid to believe in grace?* Yes, I was at first. I kept thinking to myself and hearing from others that I needed to be careful to not get out of balance with grace, using it as a license to sin. This was confusing because I had found such unbelievable peace. In my spirit I really felt what I was learning was right, but my mind fought against the simplicity of grace. This confusion went on for quite a number of months. I remember thinking to myself at one point, *The grace that some people worry offers a license to sin must be completely different from this revelation of grace that I am getting, because sinning is the furthest thing from my mind.* I'm not saying by any means that I completely stopped sinning, but I certainly wasn't tempted to sin *more* because of grace. In fact, I had quite the opposite response: I fell more deeply in love with God and His Word than ever before. Which in turn drove my desire to allow Him to live through me.

As I continued on my journey, I finally came to the realization that believers who continue in a lifestyle of sin while claiming to be under God's grace do not understand true grace at all. They are enjoying neither freedom from condemnation nor the benefits of putting their trust in Christ's power. Despite what they may say, they are still depending on their self-efforts to free themselves. If you listen to their conversations, you will hear them talking about what they are trying to do to "get free" instead of acknowledging that they have no power of their own to free themselves. This was totally me before I understood the truth of grace. I viewed myself as spiritual because I spent so much time talking with others about my current character flaws and how I planned to improve myself. I talked constantly about myself, but almost never about Jesus.

Over time I began to see the difference between counterfeit grace, which promises to try harder to do better, and true grace, which leads us, moment by moment, to place our trust solely in Christ's power working in and through us.

As I continued to let grace demonstrate God's power at work in me, I began to experience awesome results. I was responding to life in a whole new way! My family noticed a permanent change too: a new lightheartedness about me. My kids sometimes looked at me like I was from outer space. They were wondering what had happened to their other mom, the one who never had much fun.

So I knew I was onto something, but it still took time for my mind to process this revelation. As I say, I had made Christianity so complicated that believing the simplicity of the gospel scared me at first.

JESUS CAME TO RESCUE US FROM RULES

For most of my life I had viewed the Bible as a book of rules, a guidebook to achieving righteousness. Whenever I read the Bible, attended church, listened to a teaching podcast, or read a book filled with the Word of God, most of the time I came away thinking, *Okay, now I know what I need to do to grow spiritually.* Then I would wholeheartedly set out to do it. The only problem was, I couldn't keep the rules—and the reason for my failure was right there in the Bible all the time:

But those who depend on the law to make them right with God are under his curse, for the Scriptures say, "Cursed is everyone who does not observe and obey all the commands that are written in God's Book of the Law." So it is clear that no one can be made right with God by trying to keep the law. For the Scriptures say, "It is through faith that a righteous person has life." This way of faith is very different from the way of law, which says, "It is through obeying the law that a person has life."

But Christ has rescued us from the curse pronounced by the law. When he was hung on the cross, he took upon himself the curse for our wrongdoing. For it is written in the Scriptures, "Cursed is everyone who is hung on a tree." (Galatians 3:10–13)

No wonder I was frustrated to the max. I was living as if I were still under the curse of the law, trying to follow it perfectly instead of living by and receiving grace through faith. But I couldn't pull it off. None of us can measure up to the perfect standard of the law.

Please don't misunderstand me. The problem is not with the law in and of itself; the law is holy and just. But it doesn't have the power to make us holy; instead, it serves to highlight our imperfection and cause us to realize we cannot save ourselves (see Romans 7:7–13). God knew that when He gave it to Moses. But He had a plan of redemption, right from the beginning.

But when the time arrived that was set by God the Father, God sent his Son, born among us of a woman, born under the conditions of the law so that he might redeem those of us who have been kidnapped by the law. Thus we have been set free to experience our rightful heritage. You can tell for sure that you are now fully adopted as his own children because God sent the Spirit of his Son into our lives crying out, "Papa! Father!" Doesn't that privilege of intimate conversation with God make it plain that you are not a slave, but a child? And if you are a child, you're also an heir, with complete access to the inheritance. (Galatians 4:4–7, MSG)

At the right time in His perfect plan, He sent Jesus to become a curse for us, to hang on the cross (see Galatians 3:13). Then God made a brand-new covenant with us, established through the blood of Jesus. Once we believe in and accept Jesus, we are no longer under the curse of the law, but we are redeemed from it. "For Christ has brought the Law to an end, so that everyone who believes is put right with God" (Romans 10:4, GNT).

Jesus literally did it all!

Understanding this is one of the reasons my life has so drastically changed. I was in utter shock when I realized that God didn't give the law with the intention that we would keep it perfectly but rather to prove to us that we couldn't. That was some of the best news this perfectionist ever heard. I could breathe. I could *breathe*!

Day by day, in each situation, as I learned to put my confidence in God's unmerited favor toward me instead of relying on my own ability, the pressure just melted away. When I talk about God's unmerited favor, I am talking about all the good things we get that we do not deserve. Things like . . .

- God's unconditional love
- God sending Jesus to the earth to die for us and be the one final sacrifice for our sins
- the gift of righteousness in Christ that has been provided through the finished work of the Cross
- God's never-ending mercy
- the total acceptance we have in Christ
- the amazing relationship we get to have with the Father
- the Holy Spirit being our Helper in every way

Friend, I've barely gotten started! We could also list a great marriage, great relationships with our kids, success on our job, and on and on. The ways in which we receive God's unmerited favor are far too many to count. Every single good thing in our lives—all of it—is by God's grace alone, because our own righteous deeds "are nothing but filthy rags" (Isaiah 64:6).

Oh my goodness, when I finally *got this,* I knew I was home free. I'd had enough experience doing life the wrong way—trying and failing—to realize that my own efforts would never succeed. Now I saw that God's immeasurable grace meant that I didn't need to depend on my own self. No, what I needed was to begin depending 100 percent on God and His unmerited favor, based solely on what Jesus had already accomplished on my behalf.

When I finally placed my faith in the right Person, I began to notice a deep abiding peace inside, regardless of whether I did something right or wrong. Why? Because I finally *got it,* and I celebrated this truth: *No matter what I do or fail to do, I am still in Christ Jesus!* To someone who has not had a personal encounter with true grace, this may sound like sloppy living, but nothing could be further from the truth! I love how Paul describes this new reality in Galatians 2:

Have some of you noticed that we are not yet perfect? (No great surprise, right?) . . .

I tried keeping rules and working my head off to please God, and it didn't work. So I quit being a "law man" so that I could be *God's* man. Christ's life showed me how, and enabled me to do it. I identified myself completely with him. Indeed, I have been crucified with Christ. My ego is no longer central. It is no longer important that I appear righteous before you or have your good opinion, and I am no longer driven to impress God. Christ lives in me. The life you see me living is not "mine," but it is lived by faith in the Son of God, who loved me and gave himself for me. I am not going to go back on that.

Is it not clear to you that to go back to that old rule-keeping, peer-pleasing religion would be an abandonment of everything personal and free in my relationship with God? I refuse to do that, to repudiate God's grace. If a living relationship with God could come by rule-keeping, then Christ died unnecessarily. (verses 17, 19–21, MSG)

As you can see from these verses, the Bible promises us that Christ will live His life through us. Knowing this, we can kick the rule keeping out of the way and devote our time and energies to Him instead.

GOD HAS NEVER LOVED YOU MORE— AND WILL NEVER LOVE YOU LESS

What a relief to know that we don't have to worry about impressing God—or anyone else, for that matter. You are God's child, His heir, His treasured one. Nothing can diminish your true worth.

Do you find yourself breathing easier while reading this good news? Are those muscles that have been tense for so long starting to relax? Maybe you're starting to smile. God wants you to be happy, you know. You wouldn't want your kids to be tense and anxious, always worried that they're not good enough. Neither does your heavenly Father want you to feel this way.

For example, maybe you usually feel pressured when your extended family is coming over to your home for a holiday gathering—you want the meal to be perfect. Consider the release that comes in knowing you don't have to impress anyone because your heavenly Father is already really, really impressed with you. You have all the worth and value you need in Christ, so you don't have to worry about earning worth by preparing a perfect meal or about losing your worth by saying or doing the wrong thing! It wouldn't matter if you burned the whole dinner. Your value remains unchanged since it is in Christ Jesus.

Knowing that we are deeply loved by God Himself removes our anxiety over anything we do or don't do—or how well we do it. And when we are rooted and grounded in the truth of God's unshakable love, other people will be attracted to our Christ-centered confidence. When we're no longer consumed with trying to impress, be perfect, or achieve, we are more enjoyable people to be around. In his sermon series *Free* Andy Stanley observes, "Find me a Christian, find me a Jesus follower, okay, who doesn't understand what it means to be led by the Spirit and I'll find you somebody that is struggling with sin. And on the days they do good, they feel so good about themselves…they judge all the other people around them."[6]

> When we're no longer consumed with trying to impress, be perfect, or achieve, we are more enjoyable people to be around.

I know that's not who you and I want to be, so let's take a deep breath and begin to relax in God's love today!

You may be thinking, *I want that love, Sandra. I want to know beyond a shadow of a doubt that God loves me unconditionally.* You can know His love like this because "God is no respecter of persons" (Acts 10:34, KJV). He doesn't play favorites; He loves everyone the same.

This is so different from how we are trained to think in the world's system. In the world, those deemed more beautiful, more successful, or more intelligent are loved more, but God doesn't see as mankind sees. In the world, those ambitious enough to make it to the top of the corporate ladder are viewed as more successful, but God's unmerited favor is poured out on every one of His children who will dare to receive it—not as a result of their ambition, but because of Jesus. Job 34:19 says, "[God] is not partial to princes, nor does He regard the rich more than the poor; for they all are the work of His hands" (NKJV).

You don't need to perform for God, my friend. He could not possibly love you more than He already does.

LETTING JESUS TAKE THE DRIVER'S SEAT

In reading about God's grace that is your birthright as His child, maybe you've been wondering if you truly are free to call Him your heavenly Father. I want to stop right here and ask you a question: Have you ever invited Jesus to be your Lord and Savior? If not, would you like to do so right now?

I fully understand that you may have encountered some Christians over the years whose attitude or behavior turned you off to God and Christianity. Unfortunately, before I understood God's amazing grace, I used to be one of those judgmental types, disapproving of anyone whom I felt lived below my standard of morality. I wish I could go back and apologize to every person I previously judged and ask for each person's forgiveness. I'd do exactly that if I could remember who they all were, but since I can't, I'm trusting God to redeem my mistakes for His glory.

Despite the behavior of His imperfect followers, I hope what you have read so far has convinced you that God is incredibly good, He loves you unconditionally, and His arms are open wide to welcome you. John 3:17 says, "For God did not send the Son into the world in order to judge (to reject, to condemn, to pass sentence on) the world, but that the world might find salvation and be made safe and sound through Him" (AMP). Right now you can decide to scoot over and allow Jesus to take over the driver's seat of your life, simply by letting Him know you want to receive His gift of grace. I promise, you will be so happy that you did!

I invite you to pray the following prayer sincerely from your heart, and when you do, the Bible says you will be born again (see Romans 10:9–10). You will be a new creation: you will have the life of Christ within you.

> *Heavenly Father, I thank You that You are for me and not against me, that You desire a close relationship with me. I want to have a personal relationship with You, and I want Jesus to be my Lord and Savior. I repent of all my sins and ask You to forgive me. Right now I receive Your gift of salvation and forgiveness made available to me through Your Son, Jesus Christ, who died on the cross in my place to save me from the penalty of my sins. I believe His blood has completely cleansed me. I believe You raised Him from the dead as a testimony that all my sins, borne by Him on the cross, are cleansed forever. Jesus Christ is my Lord. I am greatly blessed, completely forgiven, and forever loved in Jesus' name. Amen.*

Congratulations, and welcome to the family of God! I am so excited for you! Please be sure to go to www.sandramccollom.com and click on "Jesus in the Driver's Seat," where you can read through the gospel message again and find some advice for your new life as a child of God.

Now keep reading because there's a lot more good news ahead!

7

What We Do Matters Less Than Whom We Follow

The Grace-Led Life Trades Rules for Relationship

As we saw in the previous chapter, the pressure we often feel to prove ourselves worthy and to accomplish feats of moral strength is self-imposed. It certainly doesn't come from God, who has already declared His love and acceptance of us. So why do so many of us get stuck on the treadmill of performance? As Andy Stanley says, people can fall prey to thinking, "All-right, all-right, I'm gonna be a good Christian. I'm gonna be more loving; I'm gonna be more joyful. . . . And . . . if it kills me . . . I'm gonna have self-control."[7] Notice the *I'm, I'm, I'm*. This is a definite sign that a person is not submitted to God's grace, because grace is about *Jesus, Jesus, Jesus*!

My husband, Steve, recently shared with me how a fresh understanding of grace has shifted the focus of his life over the past few years. "I always believed God loved me, but I still felt that I needed to live up to a certain standard or else He wouldn't be pleased with me," he explained. "I believed the purpose of the Bible was for me to read it, find out what that standard for a

Christian was, and try my hardest to live up to it. I would analyze myself on a regular basis to make sure I was improving over time. I was down on myself if I messed up. I would make internal promises that I would not make the same mistake again. The Christian life was basically all about me and how I performed on a daily basis."

All this sounds familiar, doesn't it? So many of us have spent too many years trapped by the wrong belief that we can and should do something to gain God's approval. But it all changed for Steve after I asked him if he would read a book I had recently finished: *Unmerited Favor* by Joseph Prince. After reading that book, Steve experienced the same thing I did: his eyes were finally opened to the truth about God's grace, and he gained peace in many areas of his life.

"Now," Steve told me, "I see everything differently. I see the Bible as God's plan for reconciling mankind back to Himself through Jesus. God doesn't expect us to live the Christian life through our own effort but through Jesus. Jesus lived the perfect life and became the perfect sacrifice for everyone's sins, for all time. So we never have to be under condemnation about our sin. All we have to do is believe in Him and receive His gift. Best news I ever heard!"

(I feel the same way—and hope you do too!)

"Since I received this revelation," Steve continued, "I've found myself more relaxed in God's love. I no longer try to perform or analyze myself to see how I can be better. It's not that I don't care if I grow or not—or that I think sin is no big deal. No, I feel like Zacchaeus. He was grateful for what Jesus had done for him. Because of his relationship with Jesus, he naturally started having a desire to do good works. He gave everyone's money back plus more.

"I have faith now that if I focus on my relationship with Jesus and not my performance, my faith will grow and good works will come out of it. It makes life simpler when you focus on one thing: *Jesus!*"

As Steve discovered, the solution to our ongoing sense of failure is not more willpower and it's not more discipline, although we'll see both of these qualities grow as a result of living under God's grace. In fact, self-control is one of the fruits of the Spirit. The solution to our failure is not found in what we do but in who we turn to for help. The secret to our success is a person—and His name is Jesus Christ.

> The solution to our failure is not found in what we do but in who we turn to for help.

The apostle Paul describes how this "who," Jesus, connects with our "do," our actions. When Christ died, we died with Him and our old sinful self died. When Christ was raised, we were raised with Him and our brand-new self was raised.

> Could it be any clearer? Our old way of life was nailed to the cross with Christ, a decisive end to that sin-miserable life—no longer at sin's every beck and call! What we believe is this: If we get included in Christ's sin-conquering death, we also get included in his life-saving resurrection. We know that when Jesus was raised from the dead it was a signal of the end of death-as-the-end. Never again will death have the last word. When Jesus died, he took sin down with him, but alive he brings God down to us. From now on, think of it this way: Sin speaks a dead language that means nothing to you; God speaks your mother tongue, and you hang on every word. You are dead to sin and alive to God. That's what Jesus did. (Romans 6:6–11, MSG)

Success in our spiritual lives isn't tied to what we determine to do in our own strength. It's about reigning in life through Jesus Christ. When I see it this way, I am not at war with myself, but instead I am focused on the fact that Jesus already won the war on my behalf! So, for example, when I tried to unwind that yarn with my teeth gritted in determination, instead of thinking, *I'd better crucify my flesh,* the very best thing I could have done was to declare, "Wait a minute. Because of Jesus, I am dead to throwing fits. Anger and fits no longer have power over me. In fact, because of Jesus' finished work, I am righteous in Christ right now, this very minute."

Do you see the difference here? One approach involves trying in our own strength; the other leads to trusting in God and following the Spirit. One finds us trying to wrestle our flesh to the ground; the other finds us simply remembering, receiving, and living out what Jesus has already provided. Remember how Paul answered his own question about who would free him from a life dominated by failure? "Thank God! The answer is in Jesus Christ our Lord" (Romans 7:25).

Once I finally understood this, I took a deep freeing breath and started to relax in His love and in His ability! The phrase *in Christ* was beginning to come alive for me and to hold meaning for my everyday life. Colossians 3:3 says, "For you died to this life, and your real life is hidden with Christ in God." This means I can live my life through Christ, through His ability in me. I have no need to try to conquer this life on my own. In fact, Jesus actually said He has overcome the world. So guess what? Since we are in Him, we have overcome the world too, through Him! This was a total change for me. A completely new approach.

Now that I had learned this, each time I had a burden of any kind, I had a choice to make: either I could try to unburden myself, or I could place myself under the grace of God to lift the burden. The same is true for you. Our burdens can be any number of things: a besetting sin, a health problem, a lack of purpose, a seemingly impossible list of tasks to accomplish, a feeling of rejection, anxiety, a bad temper—the list goes on. The point is, whatever challenges arise, we don't have to figure out how to cope with them on our own. We can live our life in Christ, through Christ, and by Christ. Thank God!

Instead of attempting to drive ourselves toward submission or accomplishment by thinking *I have to stop doing this and I have to start doing that,* we now adopt the discipline of daily, even hourly, laying down our struggles and receiving God's grace in every area. We make it our practice to refuse to try to figure out solutions on our own; instead, we honor the Holy Spirit's role as described by Jesus: "And I will ask the Father, and He will give you another Comforter (Counselor, Helper, Intercessor, Advocate, Strengthener, and Standby), that He may remain with you forever" (John 14:16, AMP).

It looks to me like the Holy Spirit is well able to lead us. The question is, can we let go and just follow Him? When we make the choice to do so, we will see outstanding results from this way of living. Our lives will be characterized by the qualities that mark every life surrendered to Him.

> But the Holy Spirit produces this kind of fruit in our lives: love, joy, peace, patience, kindness, goodness, faithfulness, gentleness, and self-control. There is no law against these things!
>
> Those who belong to Christ Jesus have nailed the passions and desires of their sinful nature to his cross and crucified them there. Since we are living by the Spirit, let us follow the Spirit's leading in every part of our lives. (Galatians 5:22–25)

This passage is not a to-do list—although for years that's exactly how I saw it. Rather, it's a description of what comes from letting the Holy Spirit lead us. It's His fruit, not ours. Our flesh seems to want to make everything into a law and a list of behavioral guidelines for ourselves, but these qualities are the natural outgrowth of our deepening relationship with Jesus Christ.

Verse 24 reminds us that if we belong to Christ—if we have received Jesus as our Savior—we "have crucified the flesh (the godless human nature) with its passions and appetites and desires" (AMP). This death of our old sin nature occurred at the time we received Jesus, when we were taken out of Adam and placed into Christ.

Let me share with you the way I viewed this passage before an understanding of God's grace entered my life. First of all, I don't think I ever noticed that verse 22 said that the Holy Spirit produces these fruits. I saw this list as a catalog of achievements to pursue, and I continually berated myself when I failed to measure up to my definition of being loving, joyful, peaceful, patient, kind, good, faithful, gentle, and self-controlled. Also I failed to see the promise of verse 24, interpreting it to mean that if I truly belonged to Christ, then I would crucify my flesh. I felt as if I were continually at war with myself and had to be vigilant in case the enemy—me!—tried to pull a fast one. Now I know that I do belong to Christ, so my flesh already has been crucified with Him, as Galatians 2:20 says. As a result of believing this, I walk in the Spirit.

Everything comes right back to what we believe. Right believing leads to right living! We've got to get our believing straightened out, but even with this, I encourage you not to think it's up to you to fix your wrong believing. Ask your Helper, the Holy Spirit, to lead you into all truth where your believing is concerned. Ask Him to help you believe as you should in every area where you are lacking.

CENTERED IN CHRIST

I wish you could meet my friend Amy and see for yourself how God's grace is beautifully evident in her life, now that He has transformed her wrong believing. I'm so glad she was kind enough to share with me her personal story of how everything changed when she got a revelation of grace:

My life as a people pleaser began in early childhood, and the vast majority of my forty-three years had been spent perfecting my performance. Sexual abuse by a close family friend evoked feelings of guilt, inadequacy, and condemnation that color my earliest memories. The constant feeling that I had provoked the abuse left scars of shame that ran deep into my psyche. My early sense of inadequacy insisted that everyone approve of me and that I perform perfectly in every situation so that the real me, who was so desperately lacking, never showed through.

My childhood insecurities carried into adolescence. I compared myself to everyone, always coming up short and certain that every glance, every laugh was directed at me. My teenage years were spent trying to prove my worth with clothes, grades, friends, and a perfect reputation. And as hard as I tried, I never felt that I quite measured up. At seventeen, poor judgment landed me in the local police station waiting on my parents to pick me up. I spent the time trying to convince the police officers what a good person I really was, even brandishing my honor society membership card! By the time my parents arrived, the officer in charge told my dad what a great kid he had and to please go easy on me.

"Going easy" meant that I was sent to church camp during spring break. I was less than happy. However, during that week, I asked Jesus to come into my life and save me. I know that the moment I asked, He came in. However, I spent the next twenty-six years convinced that my standing with God, my salvation, my ability to receive anything from my heavenly Father was based on my performance. Any mistake would cause me to run from the Lord's presence for days, weeks, or however long it took for me to "clean myself up."

My performance-based mentality led me to run blindly on a

treadmill of guilt and condemnation until I was exhausted and powerless. I was constantly focused on myself and all that I was doing wrong. At the same time, I was a perpetual rule follower—a Pharisee's Pharisee. I made myself judge and jury of everyone in my life, which often made for dismal relations with my husband and other family members.

But thank God, all that changed last summer when I heard a message that truly set me free. I had heard parts of this message all my life but never in this way. The statement I heard was this: "He who knew no sin became sin for us. Jesus became your sin. Therefore you can become His righteousness." That revelation struck my heart with profound power. Light and love from heaven poured through my weary spirit. And I began to unpack that statement with the help of the Holy Spirit.

If wonderful, sinless Jesus could become sin, then I became His righteousness when I accepted Him as my Savior. His death and resurrection paid my sin debt in full. Past, present, *and* future sins have *all* been washed away by His blood. Jesus loves me and I am righteous—right with God—through Jesus alone. He loves *me,* not my performance!

My identity in Christ is simply that . . . in Him! It has nothing to do with me. Hallelujah!

And that powerfully simple revelation shattered the shackles of guilt and condemnation that had imprisoned me my whole life. I am free through His blood, His love, His sacrifice, His grace. I no longer rehearse all the conversations I've had in the course of a day or all of the things I've done wrong. When I behave wrongly or have a bad attitude, I recognize it now, own up to it, and go directly to Jesus to receive His grace rather than running from Him as I used to do.

No amount of religion, rule following, or ritual ever made a difference. The revelation of the Person of Jesus Christ is the *only* thing that changed my life. As I focus on my righteousness in Him (even when I've done something wrong), I enjoy an enduring peace and a joy that I never knew before. My marriage is healthy and happy. My husband and I now have a love that is centered in Christ. After years of striving to manipulate my circumstances, I am now resting in the peace that Jesus alone can bring, as I entrust my circumstances to Him. Looking to Him continually, connecting myself to His covenant by praying in the Spirit, meditating on and seeing Him in every part of the Word, and resting in my belief in Him have afforded me a life I never dreamed I could experience. A life that is truly abundant. A life free of guilt and condemnation. A life that Jesus gave His very own for me to embrace. A life worth living.

Isn't God's grace absolutely beautiful? I just love how Amy's story captures the incredible freedom and peace that come when we finally lay down our rules and learn to walk in His righteousness alone.

Your Only Hope for Change

Did you notice that Amy's revelation came after twenty-six years of trying to measure up, of striving to be good enough for God? If you feel as if you've been stuck in the same rut for far too long, I want to encourage you that there is hope for change. Whether you want to see a change in your own character, your finances, your health, your marriage, your children, or any number of circumstances, there is hope, but only through God's grace. We don't have the power to bring a genuine change to ourselves or other people. Although we can take wise actions in dealing with circumstances and relationships, real, lasting change is brought about by the work of God's Spirit rather than by our striving.

Change—freedom from whatever holds us back—comes by the power of the Spirit as we behold Jesus' glory:

> Yes, down to this [very] day whenever Moses is read, a veil lies upon their minds and hearts. But whenever a person turns [in repentance] to the Lord, the veil is stripped off and taken away. Now the Lord is the Spirit, and where the Spirit of the Lord is, there is liberty (emancipation from bondage, freedom). And all of us, as with unveiled face, [because we] continued to behold [in the Word of God] as in a mirror the glory of the Lord, are constantly being transfigured into His very own image in ever increasing splendor and from one degree of glory to another; [for this comes] from the Lord [Who is] the Spirit. (2 Corinthians 3:15–18, AMP)

We are changed, transfigured into the image of Jesus, as we behold Him. But what does it mean to "behold" Him? How do we do that? Here are some synonyms for the word *behold* that might give us some insight: *catch, consider, contemplate, lay eyes on, notice, observe, regard, see, watch,* and *witness.*

Let's consider how these synonyms play out in our everyday lives.

When we take time to *notice* Jesus in our lives all throughout the day, we are changed. One way to do this is by *observing* examples of His unmerited favor, anything good that comes into our lives, from getting that parking place at the crowded mall to a promotion at work. Even if it was something we worked hard for, *consider* who gave us the wisdom, ability, and strength to accomplish it. God! *Watching* for instances of God's goodness makes us more thankful. In essence, this is what my family and I do through what we call our Book of Remembrance. We *notice* all the good things God does in our lives and record them so we can go back at a later date and recall them. That changes us by strengthening our faith.

Our hearts also cannot help but be changed when we *contemplate* Jesus' sacrifice on the cross by receiving communion. Jesus Himself said, "Do this in remembrance of me" (Luke 22:19, NIV), and as we remember all He accomplished on our behalf, we will be freed from the trap of focusing on ourselves.

Another way to behold Him is to purposely *catch* God flooding our lives with His love and His mercy. We could even say, "I caught You, God. There You go again, loving me unconditionally!"

Another way that beholding God leads to change in us is when we *witness* His beautiful creation. Not long ago I remember waking up to a beautiful Missouri winter morning and seeing wet snow resting on the tree branches. The scene was absolutely gorgeous—picture perfect—so in my personal time with the Lord that day, I looked out the window, choosing to *lay my eyes on* the beauty of God's creation. I took a photo of it, which I then e-mailed to several people and posted on Facebook. My friends and I talked about His beauty all day long. As my dad says, "It's God's painting!"

One of the most exciting ways to behold Jesus' glory is when we read and study the Bible! As we *regard* His Word, God will unveil its life-changing secrets if we ask Him to.

This understanding revolutionized my personal time with God. Previously I had spent time in prayer and Bible reading each morning because I was afraid He would be mad at me if I didn't. My time with God was meant to impress Him, not to nurture a deepening relationship with Jesus.

But as I mentioned before, after coming to this grace revelation, I started *seeing* and reading the Bible from a completely different perspective. Instead of seeing a book of rules, I now see a book full of promises—promises made available to us by a heavenly Father who, rather than waiting to punish us when we step out of line, invites us to step into His presence just as we are. In fact, at the end of this book (see page 171) is a collection of those promises for you and me to meditate on so we can keep our minds focused, day by day, on His gifts of grace.

The difference this has made for me is like night and day. I am like a little kid, basking in the glow of her Father's love. I can't wait to get up in the morning and spend time with Him. The change from rules to relationship in my life brought with it an insatiable desire for the Word of God and a hunger for God Himself. I can't study enough, I can't pray enough, I can't think about Jesus enough, and I can't thank the Holy Spirit enough. And as I do these things, they feed the spiritual fire in me.

I was involved in a small-group study at church, and it really blessed me to hear many of the ladies in the group say, "I got pleasantly lost in the Bible this week while looking up answers to my questions for our study." One remarked that she had to be careful to set aside lots of time before she opened up her Bible because she knew it would be hard to quit once she got going. I love this! These ladies were experiencing the beauty of Jesus being unveiled to them through the Bible. Guess what the small group was about? Grace! Many of these women, like me, were coming out from under the law, and as they did, the Bible absolutely came alive to them just as it had for me.

> I now see the Bible as a book full of promises, promises made available to us by a heavenly Father who, rather than waiting to punish us when we step out of line, invites us to step into His presence just as we are.

These are a few of the many ways we can behold Him and find ourselves effortlessly changed.

Always remember, we are not fighting for victory, but living from a place of victory because Jesus already provided our victory through His finished work!

LIFE IN THE GRACE ZONE

I hope I have you convinced by now that you can lead a life of victory in Christ, through Christ, and by Christ. Once you make the transition from performance-oriented living to grace-oriented living, you'll experience a greater sense of connection with God. Since you won't be caught up with yourself, your rules, or a continual consciousness of sin, you will be free to be guided by the Spirit, who will lead you into all truth (see John 16:13).

Of course, you will not be perfect—none of us are. But instead of going on an introspective sin hunt, you can now trust God to show you when you have slipped into living by your own self-efforts rather than relying on God's grace. When you do realize that you have gotten out of step with the Spirit, you can get right back in. You don't have to work your way back into His presence. You don't have to promise God that you will try your hardest to go a whole week without saying an unkind word to your family in order to regain access into His presence, nor do you have to give up your favorite hobby for the next month as a penance. These promises would merely be your trying to make a way through your own human effort again rather than trusting Christ. I really like what our pastor, Jeff Perry, said recently at Friday-night church: "The Christian life is not so much about us exerting our human effort; it's about us responding to God's power!"[8]

Once we receive Jesus as our Savior, sin no longer separates us from God. In fact, coming boldly into His presence even when we have sinned is necessary so we can "receive mercy and find grace to help us in our time of need" (Hebrews 4:16, NIV). We can humbly say to God, *I know Jesus' blood has me covered, and Your relationship with me doesn't depend on my perfection. So since I am not trusting in my own goodness, I am going to go ahead and enjoy You and trust You to clean me up.*

Each time you need help, you simply receive it. It's His grace. In fact, the Holy Spirit is referred to in Zechariah 12:10 as "the Spirit of grace" (NKJV). He's been there since the day you made Jesus your Lord and Savior. Following Him leads to freedom and joy.

Matthew 6:33 has always been my favorite scripture: "But seek first His kingdom and His righteousness, and all these things will be added to you" (NASB). Although I have treasured this verse since I was very young, I didn't fully understand it until I understood grace. The scripture says to "seek . . . His righteousness," which I interpreted to mean that I needed to seek God with all my heart and do good works. If I succeeded with that task list, then other good things would be given to me. Basically this verse sent me on a frustrating works trip.

The truth is that, for all those years when I tried to organize my days, my thoughts, and my actions in order to be righteous, I was already righteous in Christ! All I needed to do was to rest in the righteousness that He has given me—His righteousness—by meditating on it and declaring it on a regular basis!

When I first began the practice of leaning into His grace and letting go of my own efforts, it was kind of humbling for me. I was fiercely independent and found it difficult to accept that I could do absolutely nothing to earn my own righteousness. Late one night as I was reading my Bible and really seeing my exhausting works-oriented life through the lens of grace, I said out loud, "I've been robbed." That is exactly how I felt, and that is exactly what the devil intended to do all those years: to rob me. But God wanted me to experience so much more. Jesus said, "The thief comes only in order to steal and kill and destroy. I came that they may have and enjoy life, and have it in abundance (to the full, till it overflows)" (John 10:10, AMP).

Thankfully, I am continuing to learn that the abundant, satisfying, overflowing life is found in submitting to and receiving His grace in everything. Now I am more relaxed than ever before in my life.

And my prayer for you, friend, is that you'll join me in resting in God's beautiful gift of grace.

The great news of the gospel is surprisingly uncomplicated: Jesus literally did it all!

8

Leave Your
Worries Behind

The Grace-Led Life Fills Us
with Peace

Teresa's life had long been ruled by a variety of fears. During her childhood, she dutifully absorbed the message her father drilled into their family: no members of his family—whether one of his six children or his wife—were entitled to an opinion, idea, or thought of their own. "His way was the right way," she said, "and we were mocked and chastised if we disagreed."

Insecurity and fear haunted much of Teresa's early years. Her father often drove the family car after consuming large amounts of alcohol. She remembers one particularly terrifying drive home with the family after a visit to relatives. For more than an hour, her father sped down the center of the dark, two-lane winding road. Finally, about five minutes away from home, ten-year-old Teresa became overcome with terror. "I burst into loud, uncontrollable sobs, begging him to slow down," she remembered. "My dad was furious. He yelled, 'That's enough!' Then he stopped the car in the middle of the busy road, got out, and walked home, leaving us all there."

Even though she felt certain her dad had put the entire family in a dangerous situation, Teresa believed it must be her fault that he had abandoned them. After all, he was the authority figure. "I felt so embarrassed, ashamed, and guilty."

This traumatic experience reinforced her belief that it was unsafe to be truthful about her feelings, thoughts, or opinions. "I became fearful of disapproval, anger, rejection, abandonment, failure, and punishment," she said. "And I allowed these fears to rule me and dominate my life."

Teresa became a people pleaser, trying to win approval from everyone, including God, by attempting to behave perfectly in every situation. Of course, this unattainable goal burdened her with relentless pressure. The stress resulted in fractures in every area of her life. "I was constantly passing judgment on myself and everyone else who didn't measure up to my expectations. My inability to manage and control what others said and did caused my level of frustration and resentment to rise on a regular basis." Although she was a born-again believer, Teresa says she never had a moment's peace, because she couldn't achieve the flawless behavior she believed she needed in order to earn God's approval.

Then finally something changed.

"I began," she said, "to hear about a well-kept secret: the grace of God." Although Teresa fully believed that all her sins were paid in full when Jesus died on the cross and rose again, previously she'd been determined to earn God's grace and favor. But when she discovered that His grace is free, is undeserved, and cannot be earned, a light bulb switched on in her mind and heart. "By performing to try to earn it, I was declaring that His sacrifice wasn't enough to cover me—that I needed to add something more to it. This put me and my performance, rather than Him, on the throne of my life. How arrogant of me!"

Teresa confessed her sin and vacated the throne of her life so that its rightful King might reign there. And freedom, peace, and joy began to push worry, anxiety, and striving out of her life.

She told me, "I am learning to focus on Him and all He is, rather than on me and my deficiencies. The walls of self-protection are being dismantled as I allow the Lord to be my Protector." Through the power of God's grace at work in her, Teresa has found the strength and courage to share her true feelings and opinions, which has freed her to be authentic with the people in her life. "I am experiencing so much more peace now," she told me, "as I refuse to allow fear to rule me. I truly feel like a new creation!"

JESUS' OWN SPECIAL PEACE

When we go through our days believing everything depends on us—on our ability to execute each task perfectly, on how well we respond to each circumstance that arises, on how effectively our lives shine for God—stress and strain are inevitable. Although my own childhood was nothing like what Teresa endured, I certainly relate to the anxiety she felt as an adult as I tried—and failed—to control myself, my circumstances, and everyone around me.

With my grace glasses on, now everything looks different—my circumstances, my to-do list, my relationships, and especially Scripture. As I mentioned earlier, I get so much more out of my time in the Bible since I've started reading through the lens of grace.

This year I was reading in the Gospels and encountered a verse that has been one of my longtime favorites. The night of Passover, as Jesus spoke to His disciples to prepare them for His coming crucifixion, He said to them, "Peace is what I leave with you; it is my own peace that I give you. I do not give it as the world does. Do not be worried and upset; do not be afraid" (John 14:27, GNT). When I read the part of the verse where Jesus said, "It is my own peace that I give you," a revelation suddenly hit me. I thought, *Oh,*

I get it now. Jesus meant that He gave me the very peace that He lived in so that I can live in that same peace. I remember calling several people afterward, so excited to share my new understanding of this verse.

Remember, right believing leads to right living. So in this instance, my believing that Jesus meant exactly what He said about giving us His own peace helps me to really, truly live in His own peace.

Let's consider for a moment just a few examples of the peace that Jesus lived in:

- Jesus never hurried and He never worried, so that means it is possible for me to live without hurrying or worrying.

- Jesus trusted His Father implicitly, so that means it is possible for me to trust God, my Father, implicitly.

- Jesus frequently set aside the incredible pressures of life in order to slip away to spend time with His Father. This means I can prioritize my relationship with God over my to-do list.

- Jesus did not bow to the expectations others placed on Him. He kept His eyes on His Father's wishes. This means I can also live free from the tyranny of other people's expectations and follow God.

- Jesus faced trials and suffering, secure in the knowledge that the Father was in control, so no matter what I go through, I can also rest in the peace of knowing that God is with me and He will never leave me.

This is the peace we have been given, Jesus' own special peace. It is amazing how getting a revelation on one verse can change us forever.

Am I saying we can be perfect in our actions? No. I realize we are continually learning the value of relying on Jesus and allowing Him to live His life through us more and more. But since we know that right actions will follow right believing, if something is lacking in our obedience, that means something is off in our believing. In this instance, maybe we have forgotten that Jesus gave us His special peace, which means we don't have to try to produce our own peace. Maybe we have forgotten that Christ lives in us so that the very peace we need is already present and within reach. Maybe we have forgotten that we are no longer slaves to the sin of worry.

Any way you break it down, if we feel continual frustration and unease about some aspect of our lives, then we have made a choice not to live under, not to surrender to, not to receive, not to accept, not to put our faith in God's grace in that area. Part of the gospel is the peace He gives us.

I hope you are seeing how simple the gospel message is. All we have to do is continue to submit ourselves to God's amazing grace instead of living by our own efforts. But because of our minds, our wills, and our emotions— which represent what we think, what we want, and how we feel—submitting to God's grace is a decision, and not always an easy one.

This is where we turn to the second part of John 14:27, in which Jesus said, "Do not be worried and upset; do not be afraid" (GNT). Or as it says in the Amplified Bible, "Do not let your hearts be troubled, neither let them be afraid. [Stop allowing yourselves to be agitated and disturbed; and do not permit yourselves to be fearful and intimidated and cowardly and unsettled.]"

This is what submitting to the grace of God looks like: in moments when we seem to have every reason to feel unsettled or anxious, we choose instead to live in peace. We can do this because along with the gift of Jesus' peace comes the treasure of the Holy Spirit, also called the Comforter:

But the Comforter (Counselor, Helper, Intercessor, Advocate, Strengthener, Standby), the Holy Spirit, Whom the Father will send in My name [in My place, to represent Me and act on My behalf], He will teach you all things. And He will cause you to

recall (will remind you of, bring to your remembrance) everything
I have told you. (John 14:26, AMP)

Maybe you get a call from the doctor with some disturbing results from your daughter's medical test. Everything in your mind wants to start figuring out how to help your daughter get better, everything in your will wants to spring into action, and everything in your emotions wants to settle into a state of nervousness and worry. This is especially hard, I think, with negative news that concerns a child, because we parents have a strong compulsion to protect our children. But this is where you have to choose which way you will go: will you follow the lead of your own soul (mind, will, and emotions), or will you run to the grace of God and ask for help?

Let's say you choose grace. (Good choice, by the way!) Your prayer might go something like this: *God, my mind is racing right now, causing me to want to take certain actions in my own strength, and I feel like I am just about to fall apart. So I bring all of this to You and completely submit this whole situation to Your grace. As I do this, I know Jesus, who is Grace, will be Wisdom to me. I am choosing to turn to Jesus instead of allowing myself to be troubled, afraid, unsettled, agitated, disturbed, intimidated, or cowardly. And I know that because of Jesus' unmerited favor toward me, I will be filled with supernatural peace and Your Holy Spirit will teach me how to proceed in this situation according to John 14:26–27.*

Anytime the devil throws something our way to tempt us to lose our peace, we can employ this tactic of entrusting to God's grace all of our worries and concerns. I'm learning to do this every single day of my life whenever situations arise that compel me to choose between my own self-efforts and God's grace.

For years I relied heavily on rules and regulations with my girls instead of parenting from a foundation of grace. Without realizing it, I did not fully believe that God would help my girls become godly women. I behaved as if their future success and safety depended entirely on me. And my efforts left all of us feeling stressed and exhausted.

Once I started relying on God's grace instead of myself and my parenting methods to keep my kids both spiritually strong and physically protected, my frustration quickly melted, which they definitely noticed.

I am not saying we, as parents, shouldn't follow godly principles. The danger comes when we place our trust in methods, principles, formulas, or ideas rather than in God and His Word. One indicator of where we've placed our trust is who or what gets the credit when other people comment on our children's positive behavior.

It used to make me feel so good when people complimented me for having well-behaved children, and I was quick to give credit to our methods of parenting, rather than to God. I was so desperate to boost my personal worth and value that I grabbed at just about any opportunity to re-

> You have to choose which way you will go: will you follow the lead of your own soul (mind, will, and emotions), or will you run to the grace of God and ask for help?

ceive praise for myself. Although Steve and I incorporated a lot of common sense and biblical wisdom in our parenting from early on, I became prideful about my parenting methods instead of placing the credit where it belonged. I should have told people that it was only by God's grace that our girls were well behaved and pleasant to be around, and that if it was left up to us and our human efforts alone, we surely would not have the same results.

There is certainly nothing wrong with exchanging good parenting ideas; in fact, there is wisdom in this when you're talking with the right people. But we need to rely on the Holy Spirit as the best teacher in this area. He knows our kids inside and out, and when we take the time to listen, He will lead us in each situation—and often He will lead in a direction that's distinctly different from how we think we should handle the situation, how we want to deal with it, or how we feel about it. We can often recognize whether we are parenting from our own mind, will, and emotions or by the leading of the Spirit, because one results in frustration and the other brings peace.

I mean, seriously, let's think about it. Do I really have the ability to guarantee that my kids will turn out right because of my parenting, or is it God's grace that carries them through? God's grace all the way!

The more I experience God's grace, the more convinced I am that worrying is useless and trusting in Jesus is immeasurably productive.

SEATED IN A PLACE OF REST AND PEACE

You may say, "Sandra, I don't want to worry, but I just can't seem to stop." I understand because I worried most of the time, for my entire life—until just about nine months before I started writing this book. It's a journey for all of us, and as some of my personal stories prove, I sometimes find myself losing sight of what I have in Christ and making the wrong choice too. When you feel worried, I encourage you to take your worries to Jesus and talk to Him about them. Don't be afraid; He is just waiting for you to ask Him for help. God delights in answering our prayers. Even when we don't get the answer we expected, which happens to all of us sometimes, if we watch long enough, we can see God's grand design being woven into our lives.

One of the best ways to nurture peace is by reading and studying the Bible. As you spend time with your heavenly Father and explore His Word, you will find yourself relaxing in His love. If you're reading it through the lens of grace, as I've now learned to do, you'll see that the Bible reveals the beauty of our Savior, and the good news is, there is no end to His beauty!

It's a truth well worth repeating: Jesus has already provided for us everything we will ever need through the finished work of the Cross. We know it is done because Jesus offered Himself as a sacrifice that is "good for all time," and then He "sat down in the place of honor at God's right hand" (Hebrews 10:12). But check this out: not only did Jesus sit down, but because of Him, *we* get to sit down! "And He raised us up together with Him and made us sit down together [giving us joint seating with Him] in the heavenly sphere [by virtue of our being] in Christ Jesus (the Messiah, the Anointed One)" (Ephesians 2:6, AMP).

That's right. We get to sit down together with Jesus! Remember when Mary sat at the feet of Jesus to take in His teaching while Martha ran in every direction "worried and troubled about many things" (Luke 10:41, NKJV)? Jesus told Martha in no uncertain terms that Mary had chosen the better part. He loves it when we sit in His presence and receive from Him, just as Mary did. In Matthew 11:28–30, He invites us to come and rest:

> Are you tired? Worn out? Burned out on religion? Come to me. Get
> away with me and you'll recover your life. I'll show you how to take a
> real rest. Walk with me and work with me—watch how I do it. Learn
> the unforced rhythms of grace. I won't lay anything heavy or ill-fitting
> on you. Keep company with me and you'll learn to live freely and
> lightly. (MSG)

Did you notice the phrase "Walk with me and work with me"? Being at rest in God's peace doesn't mean we just sit around all day. Jesus' days were filled with ministry; He was surrounded by people and circumstances that demanded His time and attention. And yet He remained at rest, trusting wholly in the Father's love, and since we have been given His peace, we can do the same. I love the wording in The Message paraphrase of verse 2 in Jude:

"Relax, everything's going to be all right; rest, everything's coming together; open your hearts, love is on the way!"

You see, the Holy Spirit is always leading us, but we won't hear or know His voice if we are filled with anxiety. But as we choose to remain in His rest, the Holy Spirit will guide us. In fact, Colossians 3:15 says,

And let the peace (soul harmony which comes) from Christ rule (act as umpire continually) in your hearts [deciding and settling with finality all questions that arise in your minds, in that peaceful state] to which as [members of Christ's] one body you were also called [to live]. And be thankful (appreciative), [giving praise to God always]. (AMP)

In other words, peace acts like an umpire for us when we desire to be led by the Spirit. It tells us whether we are safe within the bounds of God's grace or whether we've crossed the foul line. You can have peace about something that doesn't make logical or reasonable sense, and you can lack peace even when a decision sounds good and fruitful. In either case, the presence or lack of peace is a signal from the Holy Spirit. This is exactly why people who let their minds dictate their decisions are in trouble.

You may ask, "Sandra, how can I recognize the leading of the Holy Spirit?" The main way the Spirit leads us is by peace.

Many times I sense something isn't right because I get an unsettled feeling about it. I would guess the same is true for you. The best way to discern whether the Spirit is speaking or whether you're being influenced by your own emotions and thoughts is to know the Bible. If what you are sensing does not line up with what the Bible teaches, then you know it is not right.

Sometimes, the very things about which we have an unsettled feeling, even after we pray, may be things that we end up doing in the future, but we first have to wait on God's timing. When we do feel peace about moving ahead with a particular decision, we also have to remember that if it is truly God's will, then He will give us the grace—provision, wisdom, energy—to make it a reality. If, however, we find ourselves sinking into frustration, we should stop and take notice. (We'll talk more about this in a moment.) We may need to take a step back and pray some more before proceeding.

> The Holy Spirit is always leading us, but we won't hear or know His voice if we are filled with anxiety.

God also leads us by wisdom and common sense. One of the things I consider when making decisions is whether what I want to do will take me away from a place of resting in God. If it will cause me to be so busy that I will be running around like crazy all the time, then I don't do it. When I started writing this book, I determined, *I will not write this book unless I can do it while remaining seated,* meaning staying in rest. For the most part, that has been the case, but a few times I have allowed myself to get anxious and frustrated. When that happened I just told myself, *Okay, the book is going on the shelf for as long as it takes me to remember that I am seated with Christ.*

Finally, there are times when the only way you will know where the Spirit is leading is to step out and see what happens. Take a step. If that steps works and you have peace, then take another step.

We are not perfect. We all miss the promptings of the Spirit at times. When we do, there's no need to beat ourselves up over it. We can simply get back in step and learn from our mistakes. I don't know about you, but I have wasted so much time either in indecision or second-guessing my decisions once they were made.

One of the things the Lord asked me to lay down this year was my habit of second-guessing myself. For much of my life, this tendency has been a real peace stealer. The devil loved it. Always remember, Satan is desperate to keep us focused on ourselves rather than on Jesus. He will try anything to keep us from living in the power of peace because he knows that when we are in peace, we will be led by the Holy Spirit, which always results in effectiveness.

Living in the peace of the Spirit frees me from constantly second-guessing my choices. It may mean that I will know how to handle a certain situation with my girls by His leading. I may sense His prompting to place a certain biblical value in the hearts of my children that He knows they will need to draw on someday. The Spirit may lead me to do something specific to strengthen my marriage. Also, when I am walking in peace, I am more in tune with how the Holy Spirit is leading me to minister to other people out in public.

Do I always choose the way of grace? Sadly, no. But I can honestly say that 95 percent of the time I now live in God's grace and rest in His peace. The two go hand in hand. I give God all the glory for bringing me to this place—for helping me enter my spiritual promised land of rest. I will never get over how He has transformed my life!

Once you start, you won't want to stop living this way. So many wonderful results come from a life lived in peace. When we worry and try to figure life out on our own, we miss out on the joy and certainty that come with following the Spirit. But as we lay down worry and human reasoning and instead go to God for guidance regarding the decisions we face, the Spirit will lead.

WHEN EMOTIONS GO HAYWIRE

As I said before, I live in peace the majority of the time, but not always. After all, I still have hormones. Sometimes hormones can be a woman's worst enemy. They turn on us and seem to take over when we least expect it. A woman can't explain it, and a man can't understand it. Like every other woman, I hate those episodes of sudden, unexpected emotional upheaval. Nobody likes to feel as if she has no control over her own emotions.

Not long ago I had one of these hormonal episodes, and I didn't handle it too well. But soon afterward I believe the Lord showed me the weapon I could use to fight such hostile takeovers in the future. I'm convinced that what God showed me can help you as well. In fact, the principle He showed me is what this book is all about, and I've been applying it in many other areas of my life, but until recently I never thought to apply it where my hormones are concerned. So here goes.

Regarding those times when one moment I feel fine and the next moment I don't, God has said, *Just leave the room when you are feeling bad, come and talk to Me about it, and receive My grace right then.* It seems so simple, but because I've been dependent on myself for so many years, I had never put His grace into practice in this area. Instead, as soon as I noticed I was feeling crabby, I immediately started trying to *not* feel crabby. I tried to wrestle control back from my emotions.

But, of course, trying to change my emotions in my own strength is always a losing battle. Once I realize that I am not being successful at changing how I feel, guilt teams up with my irritation, and things quickly go downhill. The devil draws my attention to everything that needs to be done, everything my kids have left scattered around, and everything Steve is not doing right. I find myself spitting out complaints and making cranky comments like "Surprise, the printer isn't working again" as I roll my eyes. (Has this happened to you before? Tell me I'm not alone.)

Of course, my moodiness creates an atmosphere of tension in the home, which is so unfair to my family. And on one level I'm totally aware of how unfair it is, which just makes me feel even worse, then things continue spiraling out of control. Eventually I calm down and apologize to my husband and kids. They graciously forgive me, but the damage has already been done.

Steve grew up in a home filled with tension because of his alcoholic dad, who neglected Steve and mistreated his mom. His childhood experience, combined with his phlegmatic temperament, means Steve is a peace-at-all-costs kind of guy. Well, he obviously wasn't fully aware of who he was getting when he married me!

Because of Steve's childhood, he learned to resist anyone and anything that disrupted his peace. So when I would start in on one of my fits, hoping for his emotional support, he would just get up and leave the room. This left me feeling rejected and Steve feeling resentful. Over the years, things grew worse. Steve had no idea what mood he would find me in each night when he walked in the door from work.

All of this changed dramatically once I started living under God's grace. I have become far more emotionally stable, as Steve will confirm. But I still am caught off guard occasionally by my emotions. And until somewhat recently, whenever this happened, Steve—who is very supportive when I am calm and peaceful—was simply unable to give me the emotional encouragement I needed. We had a disagreement about this a while ago, and he explained that it wasn't possible for him to support me when I behaved this way. He said he felt I should channel my frustration a different way.

To be honest, this made me extremely angry. I felt like I had finally, by God's grace, gotten over measuring myself all the time, yet now I felt measured by my husband, who was judging me for my moment of imperfection. I wanted him to support me when I was having a rough time emotionally.

Prior to understanding God's great and personal love for me, this lack of support from Steve would have left me anxious, certain that I just needed to be more perfect. Now that God's love had changed me, I didn't feel the need to strive to be perfect any longer. I knew that I could only be changed by the grace of God. But Steve's disapproval still made me angry. Both of us felt pretty discouraged about our marriage, but thankfully, God turned our hopelessness into hopefulness within a matter of days when He revealed to me the simple principle of leaving the room and coming to Him with my emotions.

After I came to this understanding, I sat down with Steve and admitted to him that I knew creating an atmosphere of tension in the home was not right and not fair, and I didn't take it lightly. I explained that I was ready to ditch my efforts to stop feeling what I was feeling. Instead, I determined that I would leave the room, open up to God, and receive His grace.

I have had enough experience with God's grace this year to know this is my answer, because every time I have surrendered to grace, without fail, He comes through.

The thing is, I have to make the choice to follow the Spirit when He tells me, *Now would be a good time to leave the room.* Our flesh kind of enjoys having fits. Although we're exhausted afterward, sometimes it feels kind of good to let our emotions run wild. But I want to encourage you, and myself, that the only way to live victoriously is by receiving the grace of God. So let's walk out of the room—let's choose to yield to God—even if we have to do so spitting and popping! God knows exactly how to calm us down. After all, He created us. Furthermore, He isn't surprised when we unload our feelings on Him. He loves us, and anything that concerns us concerns our heavenly Father!

Steve and I argued a few nights after God gave me this new insight about coming to Him when my emotions threaten to take over. During the fight Steve said something that made me so mad. But instead of trying not to be upset, I prayed, *Oh God, help me, help me, help me, because I am so mad at Steve right now. I need to focus on Your grace.* I kid you not, within a short time, after continuing to meditate on God's grace and placing my hope in the truth that He would turn this negative situation around, God replaced my anger with compassion for my husband. I suddenly realized, in a way that had never dawned on me before, that he likely responded as he had because of his painful childhood. God probably would have showed me that twenty years earlier, but I never gave Him the chance. I'd always been too caught up in my self-efforts, my own way of trying to make it all work out, to hear what the Holy Spirit had to say.

Well, guess what happened? Steve and I received counseling together from a mentor and friend of ours, then Steve continued one-on-one counseling for a while longer. Steve told me that, among other things, they talked about his childhood, and he said that just opening up about the painful memories of his past was so helpful. Steve is now totally able to support me when I am having an emotionally tough time.

Imagine! For all those years I'd been so anxious and frustrated about Steve's lack of support and tried everything I could to change him, but what ended up changing both of us was being willing to welcome God's grace right into the middle of our mess. I get choked up just thinking about it.

And this, my friend, is why I want everyone, everywhere, to know about this amazing free gift that is ours for the taking.

For far too long, I missed out on God's gift. But as I transitioned from placing my faith in my self-efforts to placing my faith in God's grace, incredible things began to happen, one after another after another after another. On an almost daily basis, my jaw dropped to the floor as God's grace—His unmerited favor—brought about something in my life that all the struggling in the world could never have done. You can still find me with my jaw dropped to the floor, as I contemplate the latest evidence of God's amazing grace.

The pure, unadulterated gospel of grace is the most amazing news I've ever heard, and I won't ever stop talking about it!

After reading this story you may be thinking, *But, Sandra, my spouse is not willing to get counseling, and he doesn't ever think he does anything wrong anyway. I feel like I am the one who has to do all the giving in this marriage. How can I be hopeful about that?*

I want to encourage you that God does have the answer to your situation. For twenty years Steve put up with my living in frustration and emotional instability, and I put up with his not giving me any encouragement when my emotions went haywire. Mind you, if we had understood grace at the time, things would have been so different between us. Please be encouraged that, as you enter into a new lifestyle of placing all your trust in Christ instead of your own self-efforts, God will work miracles in your marriage. Believe it, even though you do not currently see it, because that is what faith is, and faith pleases God (see Hebrews 11:6). While you are choosing to believe, I also encourage you to focus on the good things about your spouse, affirm him or her in those things, and stay in rest as you let God work on the areas where you want to see changes in your marriage.

> We can have so much hope for change because God cares about every little thing that concerns us. If it matters to us, it matters to Him.

We can have so much hope for change because God cares about every little thing that concerns us. If it matters to us, it matters to Him—but we have to believe this to receive it. Believing is our part, and the outcome is God's part!

EXCHANGING OUR FRUSTRATION FOR PEACE

Hebrews 11:1 tells us, "Faith is the confidence that what we hope for will actually happen; it gives us assurance about things we cannot see."

Many times we say, "I do believe. I believe that God is taking care of my problem." Then we go into worry mode, trying to figure out how we're going to resolve the situation. This is not believing. If we really are believing, we will be at rest. Even when our circumstances shout *Worry, worry!* in our heads, we know that the promises of God do not have an expiration date and God is fulfilling His Word. Consider what the apostle Paul says in Philippians 4:

> Don't fret or worry. Instead of worrying, pray. Let petitions and praises shape your worries into prayers, letting God know your concerns. Before you know it, a sense of God's wholeness, everything coming together for good, will come and settle you down. It's wonderful what happens when Christ displaces worry at the center of your life. (verses 6–7, MSG)

Our thinking makes such a difference in our ability to remain at peace. One person changes like a roller coaster, at the mercy of his daily circumstances. He is up when good things are happening, then down when even the smallest disappointments or uncertainties come. Another person can go through something absolutely tragic and still choose to trust God and make the best of everything. That individual has learned how to turn to God for what she needs, including healing for wounded emotions, and to rest in His grace.

Once we are living in this supernatural rest of God, the peace that passes all understanding, we certainly don't want to lose it. The more peace we live in, the more quickly we will notice when it is gone. Philippians 4:8 tells us what to think about if we want to remain centered in supernatural peace—and verse 9 tells us what God promises when we do.

> Summing it all up, friends, I'd say you'll do best by filling your minds and meditating on things true, noble, reputable, authentic, compel-

ling, gracious—the best, not the worst; the beautiful, not the ugly; things to praise, not things to curse. Put into practice what you learned from me, what you heard and saw and realized. Do that, and God, who makes everything work together, will work you into his most excellent harmonies. (MSG)

Whatever comes, you and I can rest in God's grace because Jesus gave us His very own peace. It is our spiritual inheritance, but it is our choice whether or not we will believe it.

9

God's Got You Covered

The Grace-Led Life
Pushes Aside Fear

've been blessed in my life to receive an incredible amount of love. First, from my parents, who provided a safe and loving environment when I was growing up. Second, from my brothers and sister who would drop anything to be there for me if I had a crisis. Then there's my immediate family: my wonderful husband of more than twenty years, who lives out the love walk described in 1 Corinthians 13 so well, and my twin girls, who have loved and forgiven me through thick and thin. Finally, I have so many fabulous friends who have encouraged me again and again. (A special shout-out to my Facebook friends. I believe you know why!)

Both my family and friends are there for me whenever I need a shoulder to cry on, a listening ear, a voice of encouragement, and the sound of laughter to help me lighten up a little bit more each year. Yet, despite the blessing of experiencing so much love over the years, it was the revelation of God's personal, unconditional love for me that triggered monumental changes in my life.

As heartwarming as it may be to know we are loved by tons of other people, the power of human love cannot possibly compare to the power of God's love. For one thing, human love is flawed, because we are all imperfect. But 1 John 4:8 tells us that God Himself is love, so His love is, by definition, utterly perfect. As the psalmist wrote,

> How precious is your unfailing love, O God!
> All humanity finds shelter
> in the shadow of your wings. (Psalm 36:7)

Each of us has a deep need to understand and receive God's unconditional love. Until we do, life just doesn't feel right. But at least from my experience, once we do get a revelation of God's love, that love melts away our lifelong fears. From that moment on January 2 when God washed over me with a wave of His love and grace that continues to this day, to my surprise I began to lose one fear after another.

The more of God's love I let in, the more fear went out. There simply wasn't room for both. "There is no fear in love; but perfect love casts out fear" (1 John 4:18, NKJV).

GOD'S PHOBIA-BUSTING LOVE

From the time I was a little girl, I was terrified of spiders and insects. While I was growing up, I remember we had a number of ant infestations in our kitchen and, to my dismay, one in my bedroom. We couldn't find where they were coming from so my Dad placed a piece of candy on my bed. Soon a line of ants marched right up onto my bed and back down to where they came from. It was clear they were telling all their friends to join them for the sugar party. I nearly broke out in hives when I saw them and thought I would never want to sleep in my bedroom again. Although insects creeped me out, spiders brought on a whole new level of fear—one that followed me into adulthood.

After we moved over a year ago into a home partially surrounded by woods, we began experiencing way too many close encounters of the spidery kind. One day my girls saw a spider up in the corner of our family room, which has a very high ceiling. I sure wasn't getting up on a ladder to get that creepy thing. Steve was at work, so my daughters and I came up with our own solution. We got a bunch of super balls and started throwing them at the spider. We didn't score any deadly hits, but we had a lot of fun trying. Eventually, Steve came home from work, got a tall ladder, and took care of it. Whew!

One day a technician with an extermination firm found a brown recluse spider in one of our sticky traps. When he showed me the deadly poisonous spider, I immediately broke out in a hot flash and started shaking. Needless to say, I signed up for the full extermination plan right there on the spot. I even asked him if they could spray my lawn and the woods, as I wanted to push these scary creatures as far from our home as possible. You could tell the guy was used to dealing with other irrational arachnophobes. He kindly assured me that, although they couldn't spray our lawn and woods, they would not stop until the problem was under control. The best answer, I am sure, since we were not seeking to harm the deer, squirrels, birds, chipmunks, and other animals who make their home in the woods surrounding us. We just wanted a spider-free house.

It's not as if spiders were crawling all over my home, but I couldn't stop wondering if a spider might be waiting around each corner. When I did see one, I felt almost paralyzed with fear. I didn't want to lose sight of the spider because it might get away—and the idea of a spider hiding somewhere in my home freaked me out even more than seeing one. But I didn't like killing them myself, so if Steve was home I would just yell for him or send one of the girls to get him while I kept the spider in sight.

Many months after God's transforming love took root in my life, I suddenly realized something had changed. I was walking through my basement one day and suddenly realized, *Oh my goodness! I am not afraid of spiders anymore. I am no longer afraid to walk around my house.* Believe me when I say that would not have been possible without some supernatural intervention.

I would have never guessed it, but what I really needed in order to get free from my fear of spiders was grace in the form of "God with us." I needed to know deep down that spiders are no match for God and God is always with me. God's love had so overtaken my life at this point that I just knew that He was watching over me—to protect me even from spiders. Wow, look at what right believing did for me in this instance!

When I do see a spider now, I no longer need to call Steve and I no longer break out in a hot flash or get chills. I simply trust God. And He knows exactly how happy I am to be able to walk around my home freely—without fear.

This was a huge breakthrough for me. Anytime we lose a fear, we live in greater peace. As 1 John 4:18 suggests, the more we know of His love, the more fears will be expelled from our lives. I believe it is God's will for His love to become more deeply embedded in our hearts every day so that we can continue on a path toward fearlessness.

> Take every opportunity you can to believe that God loves you and that He is working things out on your behalf.

I wonder what would happen if we were so secure in God's love that we could throw off every fear in our lives. What would happen if each time we sensed fear creeping in, we just said, *Access denied. I'm deeply loved.* I wonder what would happen if we were really free from fear . . . I think we should be the generation that finds out!

However you are experiencing fear today, I encourage you to consciously let God's love into that area. Take every opportunity you can to believe that God loves you and that He is working things out on your behalf.

FROM THE GRIP OF FEAR
TO THE GLORY OF FREEDOM

Living in fear of spiders is one thing, but living in spiritual paralysis holds far greater consequences.

Before I started living fully in God's love and grace, I endured the continual paralyzing fear that I was going to sin. As I described earlier, I had falsely believed that my righteousness came from my own good works, so in my mind, the better my performance, the greater my righteousness.

By the way, this wrong belief is exactly the opposite of how I was raised. One of the things I heard my parents talk about and teach so often was that we are the righteousness of God in Christ. So how did I go from that to being sure that I was righteous by my own self-efforts? Legalism. I just wanted to know what I needed to do and what rules I needed to follow to be a "good Christian." This mind-set was totally subconscious. I didn't even realize that I was thinking this way, so I never got around to telling my parents about it. Had they known what was going on in my mind, they would have been able to expose the lies of the devil.

I have met so many other people who also have carried the burden of legalism for years. It seems the flesh just gravitates in the direction of self, and for those of us with a temperament that leans toward perfectionism, the desire to be good just adds fuel to the fire.

Thankfully, the truth finally sunk in, little by little, as I continued on my journey of grace. That moment when I really understood that my righteousness is a gift because of Jesus' finished work and not at all based on my own works, I nearly fainted. Major relief. As I mentioned in chapter 6, I was excited to hear the news, yet at the same time, I was afraid to believe it. But once I did, I never turned back!

When I stopped going to Jesus based on my own goodness and started going to Him based on His goodness, in Him I found everything I needed, including the power to overcome temptation and turn away from sin. Now I love to sit and think about His goodness, to be still and know that He is God, to thank Him for His finished work, to receive His unconditional love for me, and to love Him in return.

I am not the least bit afraid of sinning for two reasons.

First, I now believe that Jesus can keep me from stumbling. Jude 1:24–25 says, "Now to Him who is able to keep you from stumbling, and to make you stand in the presence of His glory blameless with great joy . . . be glory, majesty, dominion and authority" (NASB). The shift from trusting in myself to trusting in the keeping power of Jesus has made a huge difference.

Second, I now know that when God looks at me, He fully accepts me and sees me as finished, completed in His Son. I no longer believe God is standing up in heaven waiting to punish me when I sin. I've learned that all the punishment for my sins was laid on Jesus at the cross, once for all. He is our perfect High Priest, holy, with no fault or sin in Him, and He offered Himself up for all time and for all people (see Hebrews 7:26–27).

Jesus provided the gift of salvation for everyone who would believe in Him. This gift includes full and complete forgiveness. The writer of Hebrews repeated what God said through the prophet Jeremiah, "And I will forgive their wickedness, and I will never again remember their sins," and then he explained, "When God speaks of a 'new' covenant, it means he has made the first one obsolete. It is now out of date and will soon disappear" (Hebrews 8:12–13).

God made a brand-new covenant with us that was cut in the blood of Jesus. One of the promises in the New Covenant is that, for those of us who have believed in Jesus for salvation, He will remember our sins no more.

You might wonder if knowing this would make us think, *All right, it's a free-for-all. Let's live it up and sin as much as we want to, baby.* But that's not how true grace works. Certainly some people will continue in a lifestyle of sin, excusing their behavior with "Oh, don't worry about me, I'm under grace." But despite what they say, such individuals do not understand grace at all. Romans 6:14 says, "Sin shall not have dominion over you, for you are not under law but under grace" (NKJV). So the person who continues in a lifestyle of sin may say he is under grace, but, as Joseph Prince observes, "He is not enjoying the gift of no condemnation nor is he enjoying the free, unmerited favor of God. That is why sin still has dominion over him."[9]

You and I don't need to worry that living under grace will cause us to be spiritually lazy and sin more. When we know full well that we deserve something terrible because of our sin, but we also know we aren't getting what we deserve because Jesus willingly took our punishment on Himself, that understanding just makes us want to live all the more for our amazing Savior, Jesus Christ. Hebrews 8:10 tells us that as part of the New Covenant, God will put His laws in our minds and write them on our hearts. It also says He will be our God and we will be His people. Wow! So why do I need to live in fear of falling into sin? The answer is, I don't.

Honestly, I can't even write about this without getting choked up. Jesus did it all, and all we have to do is believe it. Believe in His finished work. Believe in His goodness. Believe in His unchanging, unconditional love for you. Believe in His mercy. Believe, believe, believe, and it will send you down a peaceful path of righteous deeds that you could never, not in a million years, find on your own.

STRENGTHENING YOUR CORE

Along with removing my fear of falling into sin, God's grace also has erased my fear of inadequacy, my fear of failure, and my fear that I would miss something huge in parenting my girls. In regard to inadequacy, I now know that Jesus, who lives in me, is perfectly adequate and I can depend on Him to shine through me. I also know that Jesus is with me all the time, so His success swallows up my failure. And as far as parenting, God anointed me to be a mom when He gave me these beautiful little ladies. As I trust Him fully, His Spirit will lead me.

We cannot trust in our own efforts and trust fully in Jesus at the same time. We have to choose one way or the other. Until I chose correctly, my life was almost devoured by fear. Thankfully, God helped me start trusting in Jesus—His great love for me and the promise that He is with me.

As a result of God helping me address my fears, I have started helping our daughters recognize the fears in their lives. For example, if one of them starts to get frustrated because she isn't grasping a certain concept in her studies, I may say, "Let's talk about what's causing the frustration you are feeling right now."

They're starting to get it. "Fear!"

> We cannot trust in our own efforts and trust fully in Jesus at the same time.

"What kind of fear?" I ask. Then we talk things through to identify the fear of not being smart enough or the fear of inadequacy. Then we discuss how all of us are perfectly adequate in Jesus, so we can relax and ask Him to help us understand. We've had many similar conversations in a variety of situations, and whoa, is it helping! I have seen my girls' confidence go up, up, up! I am thankful to the Holy Spirit for leading me into the truth of God's love and helping me lead my kids into this truth as well.

Let's look again at 1 John 4:18, this time reading it in The Message along with the context provided by verse 17:

God is love. When we take up permanent residence in a life of love, we live in God and God lives in us. This way, love has the run of the house, becomes at home and mature in us, so that we're free of worry on Judgment Day—our standing in the world is identical with Christ's. There is no room in love for fear. Well-formed love banishes fear. Since fear is crippling, a fearful life—fear of death, fear of judgment—is one not yet fully formed in love.

God's love annihilated every one of my debilitating fears, and He continues to free me from more and more fear every day, through a revelation of His personal love for me! The certainty of His grace has done for the core of my being what strong core muscles do for us physically.

We rely on our core for just about every physical movement: bending, turning to look behind us, sitting, and even standing still. Golfing, biking, running, and swimming are just a few of the activities that are powered by a strong core. A strong, flexible core is important for balance and stability. Building up our core muscles cranks up the power in almost all of our physical activities.[10]

Similarly, when God's love powers our spiritual core, it transforms so many of our reactions and responses. It strengthens us on the inside so that we can remain stable and flexible through life's trials. When we know we are loved by Him, our posture is straighter and our spine is stronger. We spend more time fulfilling our destiny and less time trying to anxiously make sure we're going to be taken care of.

When we know we are loved by God, our confidence just soars! We find ourselves looking ahead with eagerness to see what He'll do next.

10

Let God Do
the Heavy Lifting

The Grace-Led Life Rises Above
Trials and Doubts

don't think we realize the power that gets released when we trust in God's love. When we stop anxiously trying to work out everything on our own, God goes to work on our behalf. When we stop, God starts! Even though we may not get everything we believe for, as my mom, Joyce Meyer, says, "I'd rather believe for a lot and get a little of it than believe for nothing and get all of it."[11]

Life is so exciting every day once you grab hold of God's grace, because you can literally believe in Christ's power to work in you, through you, and on your behalf—in every situation. When you do, God starts doing some crazy, awesome things.

Kim, a friend of mine, shared with me the story of how she trusted God for what seemed utterly impossible: bringing change to her alcoholic, abusive parents. From the time she was first saved as a seven-year-old, she went forward in church Sunday after Sunday with the same prayer request: that her parents would quit drinking and receive Jesus Christ as their Lord and Savior. "At that time," she said, "it seemed as impossible as asking someone for a million dollars." But then, by the grace of God, eventually Kim's parents did give up alcohol. She was convinced that her request for their salvation would be answered one day too.

After thirty years, she told me, "God won both of my parents' hearts, and I rest in knowing that the promise of Acts 16:31 (NIV), 'Believe in the Lord Jesus, and you will be saved—you and your household,' is proof that God's Word is true!" This experience of witnessing God's grace at work in and through not only her life but also the lives of her loved ones continues to nurture peace in Kim's heart. "I will not fret concerning any of my unsaved loved ones," she told me. "I will pray and trust God. I will rest in Him, for He is big enough and He is able to do whatever it is that needs to be done."

Kim's story reminds me of the wonderful promise in Ephesians 3:20: "God can do anything, you know—far more than you could ever imagine or guess or request in your wildest dreams!" (MSG). Now that's a truth that should send all our doubts packing!

WHEN YOU DON'T GET
THE ANSWER YOU HOPED FOR

You may ask, "But, Sandra, what if I believe and what I am believing for doesn't happen?" Believing is so important, but sometimes the word *faith* comes with questions attached. Maybe you have thought, *I'm afraid if I don't get the answer I am looking for, that means I do not have enough faith.* Not true at all, but the Enemy would love to make you believe this. His desire is to get you to focus on what you don't have, make you feel insecure, and shut down your faith for good.

Not long ago our daughter Starr had a painful, plugged-up ear. We prayed, received communion, and administered the natural remedies we had. We all believed that her ear would open—right up until the moment Steve left to take her to the doctor. I even told her, "Your ear could pop open on the way there," and by her smile I could tell that she really believed it.

After she left, I wondered exactly what so many others do in similar circumstances: *Since my daughter just left for the doctor, does this mean I didn't have enough faith?* I felt the Lord speak very clearly to me. He said, *To keep on believing means exactly that. Keep on believing no matter what.* He showed me that I shouldn't measure my faith by the outcome, because the outcome is not my responsibility.

Let me say it again: You and I are not responsible for the outcome. We are only responsible to do our part. Jesus Himself said, "What God wants you to do is to believe in the one he sent" (John 6:29, GNT). Jesus was referring to Himself as the One we are to believe in. So as God ministered to me that day, I knew that, even though Starr's ear hadn't opened up, I was supposed to keep believing and not let the devil shut down my believing with doubt.

> You and I are not responsible for the outcome. We are only responsible to do our part: believe in Him.

It's a good thing I listened. Immediately afterward I received a text message from a friend at a local hospital asking me to come and pray for her son. An hour-long seizure that morning had caused him to stop breathing for a certain amount of time, but the doctors and nurses didn't know what had caused it.

If I had allowed the Enemy (Satan) to shut down my believing, I would have concluded it was pointless to go to the hospital, *because my faith doesn't work anyway.* Thank God I did go, and many others from church went and prayed as well. Today this little six-year-old is alive and perfectly well. The doctors cannot explain why all the tests came back negative, but we can. God's unmerited favor!

After leaving the hospital that day, I went to Whole Foods Market. As I carried my groceries out to the car, I started talking with another customer. After a while I thought, *God, You have me in the right place at the right time right now for a purpose.* I was able to minister to that lady by God's grace and His perfect timing.

When I arrived home, I gathered my family together and shared with them what I had learned. I didn't want my kids confused about Starr not getting an immediate healing but instead having to wait to feel better until after taking the medicine the doctor prescribed. I relayed to my family the doubts I had worked through after they left and how God had encouraged me that our part is to just believe and keep on believing, no matter what. Then I excitedly told them how God had allowed me to minister to several people after Starr left for the doctor because I had not allowed the devil to shut down my believing.

These days, when situations come up that require faith, one of my girls will look at me, smile, and say, "Mom, let's believe!" So many of the things that we've believed for have come to pass that we decided to start a McCollom family tradition. Earlier I mentioned our Book of Remembrance; this is where we record the acts of unmerited favor God shows to us, our family, and our friends. Our book is filling up quickly, and we know that it is God's grace working on our behalf and on behalf of those closest to us.

I'm telling you, God has awesome plans He wants to fulfill through you and me for His glory, but to take part, we must refuse to let the Enemy shut down our believing. Keep believing!

Do you remember the story of the synagogue leader named Jairus, who pleaded with Jesus to come lay hands on his sick little girl and heal her? Jesus agreed to accompany Jairus home, but the man didn't get the results he was expecting:

> While He was still speaking, there came some from the ruler's house, who said [to Jairus], Your daughter has died. Why bother and distress the Teacher any further?
>
> Overhearing but ignoring what they said, Jesus said to the ruler of the synagogue, Do not be seized with alarm and struck with fear; only keep on believing. (Mark 5:35–36, AMP)

I love Jesus' reaction: "overhearing but ignoring." This is really what we have to do in the midst of a crisis: take in the information but not let it determine our response.

Take a health crisis, for example. I am not suggesting we ignore the treatment the doctor recommends, if we feel peace in our own hearts about the doctor's plan of action. In fact, I thank God for giving good doctors their skill, which I have benefited from personally on a number of occasions. But I pray about each scenario and make my decision based on the leading of the Holy Spirit and on what my husband and I agree on together.

We listen respectfully to the doctor's report, then in our own hearts we say, *Jesus, I know You are in control here and You are everything I need. Even though this looks bad, I believe I am healed because on the cross Your body was broken for my healing.* Then in our own hearts we say, *I don't receive this bad report.* I am not talking about ignoring reality; what I am talking about is knowing where your faith lies. Is your faith in the bad report the doctor gave, or is your faith in your omnipotent God and His promises that never expire? God's Word carries more reality than anything a medical report will ever say!

Consider what happened when Jesus spoke to Jairus's daughter:

Holding her hand, he said to her, *"Talitha koum,"* which means "Little girl, get up!" And the girl, who was twelve years old, immediately stood up and walked around! They were overwhelmed and totally amazed. (Mark 5:41–42)

THE WONDER-WORKING POWER OF JESUS

When troubles arise, we can take to heart the promise of Jesus that He has deprived this world of its power to harm us:

> I have told you these things, so that in Me you may have [perfect] peace and confidence. In the world you have tribulation and trials and distress and frustration; but be of good cheer [take courage; be confident, certain, undaunted]! For I have overcome the world. [I have deprived it of power to harm you and have conquered it for you.] (John 16:33, AMP)

My friend Cally understands the value of undaunted belief in Jesus' power. She had emergency surgery for a rare type of ovarian cancer that had ruptured internally. The surgeon removed all the fragments he could see, but the rupture meant that cancer cells came into contact with healthy cells to an unknown extent and put her in a high-risk category. In addition, this type of cancer has a high recurrence rate even when found and treated prior to rupture. Cally's oncologist said that her future was "uncertain."

Initially, Cally believed that the cancer was somehow her fault, the result of something she'd done or failed to do. And she began to act as if her healing was up to her—that she'd have to do all the right things in order to earn a return to health. She told me, "Somewhere along the line, I made my healing my responsibility rather than my response to His ability."

Thankfully, God corrected this wrong belief, enabling Cally to shift her focus away from her own efforts and toward Jesus Christ, the Healer. "I began," she said, "to truly accept that somehow, someway, it was all working together in His overall plan for me. What a relief! I could finally be still in my spirit and know that He was in complete control, no matter what."

Five years later, another malignant tumor was discovered near the site of the first surgery. Just the fact that Cally found out about it was a miracle because she had been recently cleared by her doctor, who said tests would not be necessary for another year. But the Holy Spirit led her to get an early test anyway. The test revealed the tumor, and Cally went in for a CT scan that same day to confirm. As a result, the doctor recommended immediate surgery.

Her response to this news was completely different from her reaction the previous time. Cally told me, "God helped us calmly make one decision at a time and even laugh our way through it. I cannot remember losing one wink of sleep stressing about how it would all work out. I just knew that, no matter what, He would take care of everything and everyone." As Cally's friend, I recall being a witness to this peace she walked in that surpassed all understanding.

She and her husband prayed and felt that she was to proceed with the surgery. At that point, those of us in her prayer circle of friends and family didn't stop believing, simply concluding, "Okay, the doctor has this one." No, we continued to aggressively believe she was healed, even as she was wheeled into surgery. During the operation the doctor removed two cancerous tumors and took more than eighteen biopsies.

The surgeon concluded the tumors were not new or recurrent growths but that they had been overlooked during the first surgery. But then, in the spring of the following year, all signs pointed to a recurrence of cancer, with scans revealing a new mass, this time on the opposite side. Once again Cally relied on God's strength to endure whatever might lie ahead. Miraculously, just four days later, tests revealed that all of her tumor markers had returned to normal and the mass was gone!

The doctor was baffled and amazed. What do we believe happened? We believe that the Lord took care of her this time and that He will take care of her always. Due to the high-risk category she is in, her future prognosis is still "uncertain." But Cally, her family, her friends, and I are not going to go from faith to doubt to unbelief and back around the circle again and again. We will continue to do our part, which is to believe, while we trust God to do His part.

Cally told me, "For me, the journey of learning to rest in God's grace began through trials, included a miracle in the middle, and, I joyfully report, hasn't ended. He continues to teach me new things every day and will keep doing so until the day I go home to be with Jesus." I love her perspective. Through the whole trial she has been an inspiration to many people, including me.

I love to pray and believe with my friends for their miracle, but if the miracle doesn't come the way they are believing, then I continue to encourage them in whatever decisions they need to make from that point on. A true friend will never tell another friend that he or she didn't have enough faith to get healed—or that God is mad at him or her and this sickness is the consequence. No way. That's not my God!

Maybe you have been believing for something for a long time and have not yet seen the manifestation of God's hand at work. I want to encourage you to connect your weak faith with God's strength for your situation. Remember His promise in Isaiah 41:10: "Don't be afraid, for I am with you. Don't be discouraged, for I am your God. I will strengthen you and help you. I will hold you up with my victorious right hand."

Verses like this one expose the lies of the Enemy as they reveal the character of God. The devil wants you to think you won't get what you are believing for unless you muster up enough faith. Isaiah 41:10 confirms that you can trust God to carry you through any and every difficult circumstance. Just relax in His strength.

When you feel anxious or are tempted to doubt, have a heart-to-heart conversation with your heavenly Father. He loves it when you talk to Him, and He loves it when you receive from Him. Whether you're looking for a relationship to be restored, financial help, relief from nagging pain, or the solution to a problem at work—whatever your situation, just bring it before the Lord in prayer and then act like it is as good as done. Worry doesn't do one bit of good, but faith pleases God. He loves to hear us say, "I know You've got me covered, Father God!"

GRACE UNDER PRESSURE

We are going to spend our mental energy on either believing or doubting. We will be much happier if we spend it on believing.

My dad and I were talking recently about believing, and he said, "Our minds are so finite compared to God's. He sees the big picture in our lives, which is why we should just believe and leave the rest to God." I'm convinced he's exactly right. Romans 8:28 tells us, "And we know that God causes everything to work together for the good of those who love God and are called according to his purpose for them." We don't understand why everything happens the way it does, but we can believe God is working His purposes through it all. If we can trust Him through the heartache, that painful experience may not make sense all by itself, but God can bring it together with all the other ingredients in the recipe of our lives and cause everything to ultimately work out for our good and for His glory.

Think about Joseph. Hated by his brothers, thrown into a pit, sold into slavery, lied about, and thrown into jail for sixteen years for something he did not do. We don't know what exactly Joseph went through each and every day, but common sense tells us that he must have had some pretty low periods over all those years. But he trusted God with the big picture, and the Bible says God was with Joseph in everything he did. He let God use him to minister to others right in the middle of his pain, and during those trials he let God prepare him for what was to come. Eventually, God used Joseph to save countless lives, including those of his own family.

> We don't understand why everything happens the way it does, but we can believe God is working His purposes through it all.

And Joseph is just one of many examples we could point to. It looked like Esther was a goner as she approached the king on behalf of her people, but God was with her. It looked as if Jehoshaphat and his army would be wiped out, but God was with them. They put their praise team at the front of the line, and the opposing army became confused and wiped each other out. Consider the woman with the hemorrhage, Jairus's daughter, Lazarus. God was with them all in the midst of crisis and sorrow, and He is with you too.

Someone in a small-group Bible study that my husband and I attended one evening said something that really stuck with me: "Maybe we see trials in the wrong way. Consider a pole-vaulter. He has to run down the track carrying that long, heavy, awkward pole, but that very pole, when used correctly, is what gets him to where he wants to be—to victory."

This idea echoes what we read in James about what we gain from life's difficulties:

> Consider it a sheer gift, friends, when tests and challenges come at you
> from all sides. You know that under pressure, your faith-life is forced
> into the open and shows its true colors. So don't try to get out of

anything prematurely. Let it do its work so you become mature and well-developed, not deficient in any way. (1:2–4, MSG)

Trials are a part of life in a fallen world. Trials aren't punishment for our sin, since Jesus carried and paid for the full penalty of our sins on the cross (see Isaiah 53:5). I don't believe God puts pressure on us to teach us a lesson, but He will strengthen us during hard times if we run toward Him rather than away. God does not leave us alone in our trials without comfort and help, but instead He gave us the Holy Spirit as our Comforter, Counselor, and Standby.

Blessed be the God and Father of our Lord Jesus Christ, the Father of mercies and God of all comfort, who comforts us in all our affliction, so that we may be able to comfort those who are in any affliction, with the comfort with which we ourselves are comforted by God. (2 Corinthians 1:3–4, ESV)

I have certainly seen many people live out these verses amazingly well. I am thinking of a number of situations in which I went to minister to friends during a time of need, yet the faith and peace they showed despite their terrible ordeals actually ended up being a great inspiration to me. I hate to see people hurting. I just want so badly to be able to rewind their stories and undo their pain for them. I can't even pretend to have all the answers, but I truly believe God is there in the midst of people's pain.

OUR COMPASSIONATE GOD

About six months ago a dove flew right into our window, then fell to our deck, badly injured. The dove's mate was right there with her, waiting to see how she was. He even prodded her to move once in a while, and she did try, but she simply could not.

I called the bird rescue center in my town. We did everything they told us, but the dove had a head injury and an injured wing and wasn't recovering. So I got a towel, like they told me to, picked her up, and put her in a box. Our whole family drove her to the bird rescue center. I held her box on my lap and kept a close eye on her for the entire drive. I will never forget how that beautiful dove looked at me.

When we arrived, they took her into a back room to assess her condition. Her breathing was so labored that they gave her a shot to calm her down. We returned home to wait for their call. If she recovered, they would bring her back to our house and release her into the wild from there. Sadly, she died later that day, but I was thankful that we were able to help relieve her suffering during the last hours of her life.

The concern and compassion that compelled me to help that dove remind me in a small way of how God feels toward us. He cares about us so deeply, and nothing happens to us that He does not know about. He is with us, watching over us. Jesus said, "Are not two little sparrows sold for a penny? And yet not one of them will fall to the ground without your Father's leave (consent) and notice. But even the very hairs of your head are all numbered. Fear not, then; you are of more value than many sparrows" (Matthew 10:29–31, AMP).

In fact, we are so treasured by God that He says this to His people: "For I know the thoughts and plans that I have for you, says the Lord, thoughts and plans for welfare and peace and not for evil, to give you hope in your final outcome" (Jeremiah 29:11, AMP).

I don't know exactly what God has for you down the road, but I do know that He is preparing you for it now. God has so many awesome plans for your future, and because He loves you so much, He is preparing you for those plans ahead of time. He is preparing you today for tomorrow, this year for next year, and this decade for the next one. Nothing is wasted, including those hard days when nothing seems to go right.

I don't believe for one minute that God makes bad things happen to us, such as sickness, disease, or accidents. What I do believe is that our heavenly Father loves us so much that, if we run to Him during hard times, He will use what we are going through now as a testimony to help others in the future. When we endure life's trials in the strength of God's grace, we gain the ability to offer comfort to others that goes much deeper than mere words. We bear witness to His Word and His promises applied to our experiences.

> In this you greatly rejoice, though now for a little while, if need be, you have been grieved by various trials, that the genuineness of your faith, being much more precious than gold that perishes, though it is tested by fire, may be found to praise, honor, and glory at the revelation of Jesus Christ. (1 Peter 1:6–7, NKJV)

God will use the things we believed for, and in which we've seen Him work miraculously, to give us confidence in the future. Just as David gained confidence to slay Goliath by reminding himself of the lion and the bear that God had given him the strength to kill, we also need to be ever aware of His miraculous provision for us in every area of life, every day. This way we, too, can look back, remember, and gain confidence whenever He has a giant for us to kill!

If we let go of continually fighting against and trying to control life's difficulties, and if we remain in peace and trust God, He will bring us out of or take us through anything that comes. I love these confident words of the apostle Paul:

What shall we say about such wonderful things as these? If God is for us, who can ever be against us? Since he did not spare even his own Son but gave him up for us all, won't he also give us everything else? Who dares accuse us whom God has chosen for his own? No one— for God himself has given us right standing with himself. Who then will condemn us? No one—for Christ Jesus died for us and was raised to life for us, and he is sitting in the place of honor at God's right hand, pleading for us.

Can anything ever separate us from Christ's love? Does it mean he no longer loves us if we have trouble or calamity, or are persecuted, or hungry, or destitute, or in danger, or threatened with death? (As the Scriptures say, "For your sake we are killed every day; we are being slaughtered like sheep.") No, despite all these things, overwhelming victory is ours through Christ, who loved us. (Romans 8:31–37)

When you turn to God, seeking grace and strength for your journey, He will not fail you. He cannot fail. It is impossible!

11

People Are God's Priority

The Grace-Led Life Flows Out
of Us in Love for Others

One of the beautiful things about living in grace is that, as we learn to let God love us unconditionally, we will be able to love others unconditionally. As we grow increasingly secure in His love, we stop being consumed with what others are thinking of us or how they are letting us down. We become free to love them, not because of what they are doing or not doing, but simply because we have freely received love ourselves.

The way to grow in our own personal love walk is to receive God's unconditional love into every single area of our lives. Ask yourself what areas you have fear in and what is causing those fears, and then you will know the very areas where you need to let in God's love to a greater degree. As a result, the overflow of His love and acceptance will naturally spill out to others.

For instance, maybe you struggle with the fear of not having your material needs met and it causes you to hold on very tightly to what God has given you. Others may even peg you as unkind, but the real root of your actions is the fear that you are solely responsible for providing for yourself. The writer of Hebrews revealed the right belief that will conquer this wrong thinking:

"Don't love money; be satisfied with what you have. For God has said, 'I will never fail you. I will never abandon you'" (13:5).

As you receive God's love for yourself in this area by believing God will never fail you or abandon you, then you will find yourself being more of a giver. You will no longer feel the need to hold on to your material possessions so tightly. I have a secret for you anyway: you can't outgive God. It's impossible. I have tried and tried, and I have not succeeded yet! Every time I respond to God's prompting to be generous toward someone, God is then even more generous toward me. It's crazy awesome because I get to be generous to someone else, then God finds a way to give it back to me again, and on and on we go. It's so much fun!

What Happens When You Let God Love You

For so much of my life, I focused on how I could love God better and what I could do to show Him how much I loved Him. Now my focus has changed to receiving His love for me, imperfect Sandra McCollom. What has been the result? Choosing to boast about His love for me instead of my love for Him has caused me to fall more deeply in love with God than ever before! As 1 John 4:19 says, "We love him, because he first loved us" (KJV).

This understanding of how love works—that it all originates with God—has transformed my relationships with other people as well as my relationship with God.

Consider the instruction we read in 1 John 4:7: "Dear friends, let us continue to love one another, for love comes from God. Anyone who loves is a child of God and knows God."

God is love! And as His children, we are filled with His love in order to share it with others.

Now let's look at the next verse: "He who does not love has not become acquainted with God [does not and never did know Him], for God is love" (1 John 4:8, AMP).

Maybe in the past you read this scripture and thought, as I did, *Well, according to this verse, if I don't love, I do not know God. Man, I keep trying to walk in love, but I fail every day. I've got to try harder. Maybe I should listen to a podcast on love. I need to find a method to help me love better.*

But if we read this verse instead through the lens of grace, we can reflect: *If I just get up every day and let God love me, if I meditate on His love, talk about His love, listen to songs about His love, and make sure I am listening to teaching that is full of the good news of the gospel of grace, I am going to love other people. All I need to do is keep receiving His love, even when I am imperfect. If I am filled with God's love toward me even when I blow it, then I won't live under guilt and condemnation. Instead I will, as a result of receiving God's unconditional love for me, "be made complete with all the fullness of life and power that comes from God" (Ephesians 3:19).*

Notice, I did not say "I *might* love other people" but that "I *am going* to love other people." If we are truly receiving God's unconditional love for ourselves, it is a given that His love will flow right out of us to others. The apostle Paul described how this cycle of overflowing looked in the lives of the believers in Thessalonica: "You need to know, friends, that thanking God over and over for you is not only a pleasure; it's a must. We *have* to do it. Your faith is growing phenomenally; your love for each other is developing wonderfully" (2 Thessalonians 1:3, MSG).

As I learn to live more fully in God's grace for my own life, I find myself being more gracious toward others. My husband and kids have noticed the change since I've come out from under the weight and pressure of trying to live under the law and learned to relax in grace.

SPIRIT-CENTERED LIVING

For so long my efforts had been centered on figuring out life so that I could get every aspect of it under control. My brain was constantly trying to find the perfect solutions to bring about the results I wanted. Then, because I continually found myself off course despite my most determined efforts, I forced myself to recalculate repeatedly, like a faulty GPS: *That didn't lead where I wanted. Let me try another side road.* If you asked my family and friends, each of them would tell you how mental I was, how my brain was always whirling with new ideas for perfecting myself and those around me.

To live by grace, I had to learn how to walk through the day following the guidance of the Spirit rather than being directed by my human priorities.

You see, the Holy Spirit is our Counselor, and He knows exactly how to help us. All we really have to do is follow His lead, which always takes us in the right direction. He won't lead us into sin, and He won't lead us to do something that is against the will or the Word of God. Here's how Jesus described the role of the Holy Spirit: "When the Spirit of truth comes, he will guide you into all truth. He will not speak on his own but will tell you what he has heard. He will tell you about the future" (John 16:13). That kind of daily guidance is a very good thing.

In the months after I began to grasp the fullness of God's grace, He enabled me to shut down my worried, hurried thoughts and become a good listener so I could enjoy the benefits of hearing the Spirit. Every day, as before, I would have my long list of jobs to accomplish, but instead of following the list, I followed the Spirit. As a result, I often found myself at the end of the day looking back over events and thinking with a smile, *There is no way in the natural that I could have accomplished all of this today.*

As I learned to lean on the Holy Spirit for help, I saw what I considered to be miracles in my schedule. Somehow the Holy Spirit helped me accomplish everything on my list and more besides. It left me shaking my head day after day. My brain couldn't figure out how everything was getting done.

When I stopped living strictly by my list and instead let the Holy Spirit lead me, I seemed to get more accomplished than I even expected. That is saying a lot because I've always had extremely high expectations—which is what so often left me disappointed at the end of the day when I tried to do everything myself. But the Spirit-led life is unbelievably more productive than letting our minds lead the way. You can quote me on that.

I want to make something clear here. The fact that I started living my day by the Holy Spirit's leading doesn't mean I stopped using my brain. God gave us our brains and wants us to use them. But it was never His desire for them to rule our lives; instead, our minds are to be subservient to the Spirit.

I still begin each day with a plan and a mental list, but my life isn't centered around them any longer. I want to experience the adventure of living led by the Spirit. I want to watch as He leads me right to a person who needs someone who is willing to stop, ditch the day's plan if need be, and share the love of Jesus.

> When I stopped living strictly by my list and instead let the Holy Spirit lead me, I seemed to get more accomplished than I even expected.

Certainly over the years I've often interrupted my daily tasks to minister to individuals in need of God's hope. I've always had a heart to help people, but before God's grace took over, my mind wouldn't let me linger for too long. It would remind me, *We have things to accomplish, remember? We've gotta get those check marks on our list.*

But now I live for these Spirit-led encounters. And I'm confident you'll find this a more rewarding way to live as well!

God has a calculated purpose for your existence, a grand plan for you to be part of changing the destinies of many with His grace. Your part is to believe that He has placed within you His ability and anointing to advance His kingdom for His glory.

Life ceases to be a drudgery and begins to be an adventure when you see your true purpose, a purpose far beyond checking off items on your to-do list each day.

- Every time you encourage your child to embrace a godly value within his heart, you help equip your child for times of decision.
- Every time you honor your husband or encourage your wife, affirming your spouse's value, you help provide inspiration needed to fulfill your spouse's destiny.
- Every time you tell your friends that you are behind them and believe in them, you have just been used by God to help propel them to the next level He has for them.
- Every time you serve your parents or take care of your elderly relatives, you demonstrate God's tender care for them.
- Every time you look a complete stranger in the eyes and declare how much God cares about everything that concerns that individual, you have just demonstrated that God loves that person so much that He will pull that person out of a crowd, if need be, to make His love real to him or her.
- Every time you forgive and show mercy to those who know full well they don't deserve it, you are revealing the compassionate heart of God.
- Every time you walk in the way of love, joy, peace, patience, kindness, goodness, faithfulness, gentleness, and self-control, the possibilities are endless.

You are highly significant in God's design! Your life was created to give Him glory.

Let's invite Jesus into every part of our lives and accept everything He died to provide for us, so we can get past ourselves and make great strides in the kingdom of God for His glory!

When the Holy Spirit leads our lives, we go to the exact places God wants us to go. As we start seeing what He wants to accomplish, our own desires fade away. We care less about our to-do lists and more about our Spirit-led assignments. We want to carry God's compassion to the world, starting with our own families. We want to be expressions of His hope, speaking God's words of encouragement to people. We want to be ambassadors of His love, stopping each time He nudges us to minister in caring ways to the people He created.

You and I are to be deliverers of God's grace, ministers of His covenant, heralds of His promise of abundant life. "He has enabled us to be ministers of his new covenant. This is a covenant not of written laws, but of the Spirit. The old written covenant ends in death; but under the new covenant, the Spirit gives life" (2 Corinthians 3:6).

Getting out of my brain and living by the leading of the Holy Spirit has been, hands down, one of the most freeing things I have ever experienced. I just laugh inside now when my brain screams out, *Do it my way; I won't let you down.* I think, *You may as well be quiet, brain. You are no longer my leader but my servant. I have a new leader: the Holy Spirit!*

The great news is that the more deeply we are rooted in God's love for us, the easier it is to share it. I am able to be a witness for Christ far more often now than when I was seeking to earn more check marks on my spiritual to-do list in an effort to please God. I now take time to feast on the love of God for myself every day, and every day I feel stronger in the core of my being. His love in me just bubbles right out of me to others without my having to make a plan for it. I get up each morning and believe that God will have me in the right place at the right time to encourage the right people. Then I stay open to following the leading of the Holy Spirit.

Galatians 5:25 says, "If we live in the Spirit, let us also walk in the Spirit" (NKJV). To "walk in the Spirit" simply means that we stay in step with God. I love this, and I love knowing that the Holy Spirit, our Helper, will even help us stay in step!

BECOMING A HOUSEHOLD OF GRACE

I think it is safe to say that, more than anything else, those of us who are parents want our kids to feel loved by us, and loved by God through us, each and every day. In the past, while finding my way through the parenting maze, I admit that many times I failed to consult my Counselor, the Holy Spirit, as I should have. As a result, the balance in our household too often tipped away from compassion and toward legalism.

As my husband and I began getting a revelation of God's grace toward us personally, we sat down with our girls and told them specifically what we were learning about how much God loved all of us. Of course, we had told them before about God's love, but now we sat down together as a family and I told them specifically how God's love was changing me personally, which they already had a clue about from having witnessed the increased peace in my life. I apologized to each of my girls and to my husband for treating them as I had in the past. I knew I had quite a bit of undoing ahead of me in order to repair the damage I had caused to our relationships. I could honestly tell them that I'd been unaware of the deception that I'd been living in, but by God's mercy, now my eyes were opened and things would change for all of us.

I could actually see the stress fade from our girls' faces as we started making a big deal about God's love for them. Let me interject something here: do you know it is impossible to talk to your kids too much? We talk about everything in the McCollom house, and our girls feel safe with us emotionally and in every other way. But before I knew the unconditional love of God for myself, that wasn't the case. I never physically abused my kids, but they didn't feel totally safe emotionally with me because they didn't always know how I was going to react in any given situation. I had to build this environment of trust over time by showing them that they were truly safe with me.

One morning soon after we sat down and talked with the girls, they were excited to share some of the details they had learned from their history assignment the previous afternoon. Starr started telling me one thing after another after another. Abruptly, she stopped, looked at me kind of funny, and said, "Is it okay if I just tell you one more thing?" I could see that she was anticipating the reaction of the old mom.

In the past, as a result of trying to get my worth and value from checking off my list every day, there were frequent occasions when I was too busy to hear what my girls had to say. Sad but true. Yes, I spent plenty of time with them and listened to them, but my body language often expressed how rushed I felt. Mom had things to accomplish.

So on this particular morning, I said to Starr, "Let me stop you right there, because I see that you are reacting to the old mom. I am not her any longer. You do not have to be fearful that you are taking too much of my time. I value you, and I want to hear everything you want to say to me." This put a smile of relief on her face.

Sometimes we have to undo things we did in the past, because our mistakes have created fearful reactions in our friends or family. But anything can be undone by God's grace, and we don't even have to feel guilty about these things. Of course, the devil would delight in holding us back with condemnation or lying to us that we have ruined our kids for life, but this is just another opportunity to ignore the devil, look away from ourselves, and thank God that He makes up for everything we lack. Another opportunity to be occupied with everything Jesus is instead of being occupied with everything we are not!

OCCUPIED WITH CHRIST

Of course, sometimes we spend our energy obsessing not on our shortcomings and past mistakes but on how the people around us fall short.

One of my favorite things about my pastors, Pastors Jeff and Patsy Perry, is that they are always encouraging the church to walk in love and not be judgmental toward other people, including unbelievers. Remember, sinners loved to hang around with Jesus, and they didn't feel judged by Him. They felt loved. If we really want to lead people to Jesus, then we need to love people as He did. We would be well served by taking time to look at the stories of Zacchaeus the tax collector (see Luke 19:1–10) and the woman with the alabaster box (see Luke 7:36–50) to study how Jesus treated these sinners.

If people really knew how good God is and how much He cares for them, they would absolutely be running toward Him. Sadly, too many of us act like modern-day Pharisees, convinced that we have cornered the market on pleasing God. I used to be a class-A Pharisee myself.

A number of months ago I heard a Christian say something extremely mean about another Christian. This made me so mad that I felt like smoke was coming out of my ears. As I was venting to my husband about this situation, I felt the Holy Spirit gently remind me that I'd been self-righteous, hypocritical, and judgmental myself, for many years of my life. In my case, it was because I was legalistic with myself, and as a result, I had a pharisaical attitude toward others.

My problem wasn't gossiping so much as an underlying attitude of judgment. I would do things like roll my eyes at my husband when he wasn't looking, because he failed to follow one of my many rules. I would never have said it out loud, but my hidden thought was something like, *You don't do things the way you should, and you certainly don't do them as well as I do.* Back then I also needed to learn what the word *mercy* meant in my parenting. Angel and Starr felt the pressure of failing to measure up to my totally unrealistic standards. Instead of thinking up rules and enforcing them, I would have been much better off spending my time encouraging my kids to have a close, personal relationship with their heavenly Father, because we become like who we hang around. Heart change, not behavior modification, produces real spiritual fruit, but I didn't know this at the time, and I certainly wasn't practicing it in my own personal life—until God's amazing grace grabbed hold of me.

I am so thankful that God dealt with me immediately in my anger that day, reminding me that I came from the same place as that person I was angry with. I am certainly not saying that it was okay for this other person to be a hypocrite, but I could have taken the high road by having mercy and praying for this individual, just as Jesus does for us when we sin. "Who then will condemn us? No one—for Christ Jesus died for us and was raised to life for us, and he is sitting in the place of honor at God's right hand, pleading for us" (Romans 8:34).

Yes, Jesus spoke in no-nonsense, straightforward terms to the Pharisees, but He never talked about them behind their back. In fact, try to even imagine Jesus standing off to the side whispering in His disciples' ears about the Pharisees. You can't, because He wouldn't and He didn't! I reminded myself that day that just because God is helping me understand a revelation of His grace, I don't want to become prideful and start pointing my finger at other people, nor do I want to forget that I still have a whole lot to learn.

All of us are on a journey, and none of us have a full grasp of God's grace, which is why we need to remember what Paul and Barnabas said to their listeners after sharing the good news of salvation and forgiveness of sins through Jesus: "And the two men urged them to continue to rely on the grace of God" (Acts 13:43). If we don't heed this wisdom, we will find ourselves struggling to overcome a lifestyle of sin once again.

My husband recently heard a message in which the teacher warned us against becoming grace snobs, judging everyone else now that we have this newfound grace. I thought this was a really good point. God, by His mercy, has caused us to walk in this new, restful way of living, but He hasn't appointed us to be His grace police! A true revelation of grace in a person's life will make that individual more gracious, not more judgmental.

The Bible tells us that, when it comes to our relationships with other people, we are to clothe ourselves in humility because "God resists the proud, but gives grace to the humble" (1 Peter 5:5, NKJV). Humility is not a matter of being hard on ourselves, continually concerned with our failures and shortcomings. While reading Joseph Prince's book *Unmerited Favor,* I learned a definition for *humility* that has really stuck with me: "True humility is to be occupied with Christ."[12]

If I am self-occupied, worried about what everyone else thinks of me or how I compare with others, then I will react out of the fear of inadequacy. If I am occupied with Christ Jesus, then I will be able to react with gentleness and humility, without the pressure of worrying about how I'm perceived or how I measure up.

The apostle Paul tells us, "In whatever you do, don't let selfishness or pride be your guide. Be humble, and honor others more than yourselves" (Philippians 2:3, ERV). I'm certainly not trying to rewrite the Bible, but for the sake of a teaching experiment, when reading the passage, replace the phrase "be humble" with "be occupied with Christ" and see if it helps increase your understanding of humility. You can do this with any verse that has the word *humility* in it.

When self exits the equation, Christ enters. This is great news for us because Christ is perfectly able! Whereas we might struggle endlessly to come up with ways to stop thinking about self, when we become Christ-occupied, our focus changes without our even trying. Instead of striving in our self-efforts not to be selfish or prideful, we can go boldly to the throne of grace and receive the power of God to walk in humility (to forget about ourselves and be occupied with Christ). When we embrace an attitude of humility through God's grace, we won't have a desire to be selfish or prideful because

> If I am occupied with Christ Jesus, then I will be able to react with gentleness and humility, without the pressure of worrying about how I'm perceived or how I measure up.

we are too occupied with Christ. It is actually just coming at everything from a totally positive standpoint. Bring in the positive—in this case, humility, or being occupied with Christ—and it will crowd out the negative.

FRESH PERSPECTIVE FOR CHALLENGING SITUATIONS

Occupying ourselves with Christ and learning to be led by the Spirit make such a difference in how we approach situations that arise in our parenting, in our marriage relationship, with friends, or with coworkers. I gained amazing insights into my relationships when I started stepping away from each situation that needed to be dealt with and waited to see how the Spirit directed me to proceed. With my personality I tend to want to solve problems right away instead of waiting, but lately I have been finding out God's ways often lead to very different approaches from ways my mind would have chosen to handle a situation. When I respond His way, the results I get are oh, so sweet!

For example, some time ago we made a rule that any schoolwork Angel and Starr didn't finish during their school day had to be finished that night. As a result, we were working all day, then on into most evenings, trying to regain ground lost to distractions, arguments, attitudes, or other situations that arose. I could have kept nagging them all throughout the day to get back to work, and we probably would have gotten done more quickly, but I felt that they were old enough to take the responsibility to do their schoolwork without my standing over them every second. They were not taking that responsibility most days, so it seemed as if we never had a break from the schoolwork. As a result, our family became increasingly frustrated. One night I was bawling my eyes out, so tired of it all. After I stopped crying, the Lord helped me realize that I had fallen back into the mode of placing rules on the girls in an effort to make things go the way I thought they should. I knew in that moment God was directing me to lift that rule.

Steve and I then let Angel and Starr know that we simply expect them to do the best they can each day, and if they just do that, we're confident it will all work out by the end of the week. We also told them that school will start around 9 a.m. and it will end at 4 p.m.—earlier if they finish their work. But they will not have to work in the evening.

I kid you not, the day after we lifted the rule, the girls finished, not one day, but almost two days of schoolwork in six hours, with no arguments and only one minor attitude adjustment. They were extremely focused, and all of us were much more relaxed. Our accomplishing so much so quickly was a first for sure, and I'm convinced it was not a coincidence: it was God showing me once again that the law doesn't have the power to change us, but God's grace does! "The strength of sin is the law" (1 Corinthians 15:56, NKJV).

Making everything into a rule just causes the flesh to want to disobey the law more.

There certainly has been a lot more laughter in our home since I relaxed again and chose the way of grace over rules. I am so thankful to Jesus!

I need to point out that, when I felt led to go in this direction, it did not make logical sense to me. In fact, my brain was fearfully screaming, *Well, I just can't do that because the work has to get done!* But I knew in my heart what I was supposed to do. It has all turned out right because my husband and I listened to the leading of the Holy Spirit for that specific situation.

This doesn't mean He would lead everyone to do exactly the same in similar situations, nor does it mean He might not later direct us to make another adjustment within our family's routine. We all are privileged to have the Holy Spirit in our lives to guide and direct us as individuals. If we are listening, we will notice that in relationships the Holy Spirit leads us in a certain way one time and in a completely different direction another. Why? Because He perfectly knows those involved in the relationship. He knows their pasts, what is happening in their lives right now, and what is coming in their futures. He knows their personalities, including their weaknesses and strengths. He also knows how they have been hurt in life.

When we face difficult situations in our relationships with an attitude of grace, a heart overflowing with God's love, and a desire to follow the leading of the Holy Spirit, we will find ourselves responding in ways that never before would have occurred to us—and the results will bring greater peace to our own lives and to the lives of the people we encounter.

SHIFTING THE FOCUS

As we live in ongoing awareness of the grace and the love God lavishes on us, it changes our behavior toward those around us, particularly when they fall short of our expectations. We recognize how much we depend on grace ourselves, so we feel compelled to be more generous to others, who are just as human.

Such an appreciation for God's grace in her own life has utterly transformed my friend Donna's approach to her interactions with other people.

Donna grew up in a home where the fear of God was the driving factor in every aspect of faith, and where she was frequently reminded of her status as nothing more than a lowly sinner. As an adult, she immersed herself in church activities, volunteering for every activity and attending every service. She told me, "I loved the sense of belonging, yet I still felt like a failure inside, as if I was never good enough."

That sense of failure intensified with the end of her nineteen-year marriage. *How could this happen?* she wondered. *I did all the right things and more than was expected of me.* Though she never lost her trust that Jesus held her in the palm of His hand, she continued striving, trying to get life "right." "I attended church regularly, volunteering in most everything, in my heart trying to please God or get His attention to bring me the perfect man or solution for my happy ending."

When she went to work for a ministry organization, Donna was determined to do everything exactly by the rules. She attributed her promotions to her hard work and faithful service for God. Eventually she became the manager of her department. "My focus was working hard for the ministry to get the job done," she said. "I was a person who made sure every moment was spent wisely by everyone who worked for me. I used to watch how the progress was going from my laptop before I even got to work." Looking back, she can see that her actions fostered a spirit of condemnation within the office and left everyone burdened with the demands of trying to perform up to her expectations.

Then a few years ago, while watching television, she heard a message on the subject of God's grace. "I had heard about God's grace and thought I understood it," she said, "but not like this. I learned that I had received grace the day I received Jesus but I had been living my personal and work life following the law."

Donna took the message to heart and embraced a grace way of thinking in every area of her life. Here's how she described the change: "I began to relax in Him and receive His joy. I learned that God loves me now, right where I am, not for what I will become. He is the One who changes me when I seek Him and spend time in His presence."

Instead of striving in her own strength, she has learned to rest in God's power at work in her life. "As I spent more time with God, reading His Word and asking Him to change me, He did—and He still does. I've noticed that I am responding to people and situations differently than I ever have before. At home, I love my children more right where they are, not only if they are living up to my expectations or fulfilling my dreams for them. I keep in mind that is how God loves me."

Her fresh understanding of grace and God's unshakable love for her has resulted in changes in Donna's work relationships as well. "I communicated to my department for them to work unto God's grace and love for them. The atmosphere now is noticeably different and light. I spend very little of my time with people issues and more on how to make sure they feel a part of the team, accepted, and that they all contribute with their individual gifts and talents."

Instead of continually focusing on her performance, Donna has centered her heart on the truth of God's unchangeable love for her. "So many times I think about the past and how I used to overreact to things. Now I have more joy and peace inside than I ever experienced before. Any time I begin to feel negative or fearful, I run back to spending time reading the Bible or listening to praise and worship music. The peace returns as I am drawn into His loving-kindness and His peaceful presence."

Donna's story highlights a powerful truth for any of us who find ourselves frustrated with the choices of the people around us and tempted to believe that everything would be better if we had free rein to set things straight: "He alone performs great miracles" (Psalm 136:4, GNT). It's not our job to force other people to follow the path we deem best. Only His wonder-working grace can accomplish His perfect purposes.

And in the meantime, we have the privilege of letting His grace and love flow through us to them.

12

You Can't Argue with Results

Experience the Exhilaration of the Grace-Filled Life

Results . . . It's what everyone is looking for in life. Whether you're a stay-at-home mom who wants to see that pile of laundry cleaned, folded, and put away by the end of the day or the CEO of a company who wants to feel a little less buried by work by the end of the week. But it isn't until you recognize that Jesus in you is everything you will ever need that you start seeing real results.

When your growing relationship with Jesus is the central focus of your life, you'll stop feeling the need to measure your daily success by your results, and at the same time, as you continue to receive the unmerited favor Jesus so freely offers, you will see better results than ever.

My definition of *success* is knowing that Jesus is with me all the time. That's it. End of definition!

Jesus can take you and me places we've never dreamed of, and the best thing about living in grace is that we can completely rest in and enjoy Him while He brings His will to pass in our lives. We don't even have to be concerned with how everything is going to come together. As we simply continue to enjoy Jesus, He will close doors that were never intended for us to walk through and open doors no person can shut!

Seriously, if I told you all the details of how this book came to be, I believe it would leave you speechless. It started with my finally coming to the end of myself in December 2011 and God washing over me with His love on January 2, 2012. He led me out on a journey to discover the riches of His grace, directing me to every book, every teaching, every conversation from which He wanted me to learn more along the way. Then my husband said to me out of the blue one day, "You should write a book," and God spoke to my heart a month later, confirming that He wanted me to write a book, even in the midst of my already-busy schedule, and have it ready for His timing. I remember reading the first chapter to my family, a chapter I'd written without any struggle despite being a first-time author. Tears streamed down my face as we all looked at each other and asked, "How did that happen?" And all of that led up to the miracle of how God connected me with my publisher. Certainly none of this happened because of anything I have done. I hope it's crystal clear to you, as it has been to me, that it has been 100 percent Jesus and that there is *no way to live* other than to place our faith in His unmerited favor!

I love having Jesus in the driver's seat of my life. Although sometimes He makes a turn that I didn't foresee, stops when I thought we were moving forward, or takes a detour I never expected, I fully trust Him to lead me through this journey called life.

I lived the other way for most of my life, with me in the driver's seat and Jesus as the passenger. I caused so many wrecks it was unbelievable. It's so much more relaxing to just go along for the ride and enjoy the scenery, windows down, a nice breeze blowing on me.

Of course, there are still times when I become afraid and think about taking over in a certain area of my life, but remembering the drastic difference that came since the first day I really let Jesus drive makes me realize once again that anything other than Jesus in the driver's seat won't get me to the destination that He laid out for me before the beginning of time.

> There is *no way to live* other than to place our faith in His unmerited favor!

Friend, won't you join me on the adventure of a lifetime? Let Jesus take you on the ride of your life. As you leave behind your burdens of anxiety and frustration to travel in the comfort of His love, you'll find your eyes opening to a brand-new, incredible life filled with rest and relaxation. You'll find the abundant, satisfying life that Jesus died to give you.

And I promise, you'll never regret it!

God's Promises
to Live By

In this book I have encouraged you time and again not to depend on yourself but to depend on Jesus, who is Grace. One of the best ways I've found to stay focused on Jesus is to focus on His promises.

What follows is a list of promises you can focus on as you allow the good news of God's grace to replace your old ways of thinking. This list is by no means exhaustive, but it will give you a strong dose of positive truth to meditate on. To *meditate on* something means to roll it over and over again in your mind. Over time, as you think on these promises, you will form new mind-sets that will transform how you approach life.

For example, when you are afraid, meditate on Psalm 91:9–12. Soon it will become your mental default in worrisome situations. Instead of getting pulled down by all the "what-ifs," you will find yourself believing and speaking out this promise about God's protection over you.

Hebrews 4:12 declares, "The word of God is alive and powerful." In the book of Isaiah, God says His word shall not return void but it shall accomplish that which He pleases and purposes (see 55:11, AMP). I want you to know these wonderful promises because they are for you—your personal gifts of grace from the hand of God.

So take these promises to heart, and as you do, they will become your default too!

———

The Promise of What Jesus Finished on Your Behalf on the Cross

He was despised and rejected and forsaken by men, a Man of sorrows and pains, and acquainted with grief and sickness; and like One from Whom men hide their faces He was despised, and we did not appreciate His worth or have any esteem for Him. Surely He has borne our griefs (sicknesses, weaknesses, and distresses) and carried our sorrows and pains [of punishment]. . . . But He was wounded for our transgressions, He was bruised for our guilt and iniquities; the chastisement [needful to obtain] peace and well-being for us was upon Him, and with the stripes [that wounded] Him we are healed and made whole. . . .

He was oppressed, [yet when] He was afflicted, He was submissive and opened not His mouth; like a lamb that is led to the slaughter, and as a sheep before her shearers is dumb, so He opened not His mouth. . . . And they assigned Him a grave with the wicked, and with a rich man in His death, although He had done no violence, neither was any deceit in His mouth.

—Isaiah 53:3–5, 7, 9 (AMP)

Promise in Action

- When you feel rejected, remember that Jesus was rejected for you. You are accepted!
- When you feel hated, remember that Jesus was despised for you. You are loved!
- When you feel neglected, remember that Jesus was forsaken for you. You are wanted!
- When you feel guilty and condemned, remember that Jesus was wounded for your transgressions and bruised for your guilt. You are forgiven!

- When you feel depressed, remember that Jesus carried your sorrows. He is your joy!
- When you feel oppression on your mind, remember that Jesus took the chastisement needful to obtain your peace. You are free!
- When you feel sick, remember that with the stripes that wounded Jesus, you have been made whole. You are healed!

The Promise of Salvation

But God—so rich is He in His mercy! Because of and in order to satisfy the great and wonderful and intense love with which He loved us,

Even when we were dead (slain) by [our own] shortcomings and trespasses, He made us alive together in fellowship and in union with Christ; [He gave us the very life of Christ Himself, the same new life with which He quickened Him, for] it is by grace (His favor and mercy which you did not deserve) that you are saved (delivered from judgment and made partakers of Christ's salvation).

—Ephesians 2:4–5 (AMP)

Promise in Action

- When you feel dead in your sin, remember that God made you alive in relationship with Christ. You are saved!

The Promise of No Condemnation

So now there is no condemnation for those who belong to Christ Jesus.

—Romans 8:1

Promise in Action

- When Satan tries to bury you under condemnation, remember there is no condemnation for you when you are in Christ. You are released!

The Promise of the Holy Spirit

But the Comforter (Counselor, Helper, Intercessor, Advocate, Strengthener, Standby), the Holy Spirit, Whom the Father will send in My name [in My place, to represent Me and act on My behalf], He will teach you all things. And He will cause you to recall (will remind you of, bring to your remembrance) everything I have told you.

—John 14:26 (AMP)

Promise in Action

- When you lack the strength, wisdom, or ability to accomplish a certain task, remember that God sent you a Helper, the Holy Spirit. He is able!

The Promise That Jesus Made the Final Sacrifice

But our High Priest offered himself to God as a single sacrifice for sins, good for all time. Then he sat down in the place of honor at God's right hand.

—Hebrews 10:12

Promise in Action

- When you are tempted to carry the guilt for your sins or to somehow earn forgiveness, remember that Jesus was the one final sacrifice. It is finished!

———

The Promise of Eternal Life

For the Lord himself will come down from heaven with a commanding shout, with the voice of the archangel, and with the trumpet call of God. First, the believers who have died will rise from their graves. Then, together with them, we who are still alive and remain on the earth will be caught up in the clouds to meet the Lord in the air. Then we will be with the Lord forever.

—1 Thessalonians 4:16–17

Promise in Action

- If you are getting weary of this life, remember, Jesus is coming back for you. Someday you will be with Him forever!

———

The Promise of Protection

Yes, because GOD's your refuge,
    the High God your very own home,
Evil can't get close to you,
    harm can't get through the door.
He ordered his angels
    to guard you wherever you go.

—Psalm 91:9–11 (MSG)

Promise in Action

- If you feel afraid, remember that God is with you everywhere you go. He is your shield!

———

The Promise That God Wrote His Laws on Your Heart When You Became His Child

This is the new covenant I will make with my people on that day, says the LORD: I will put my laws in their hearts, and I will write them on their minds.

—Hebrews 10:16

Promise in Action

- If you feel insecure about your ability to live as a child of God, remember that His laws have already been written on your heart. He is your wisdom!

———

The Promise of God's Mercy

Then he says, "I will never again remember their sins and lawless deeds."

—Hebrews 10:17

Promise in Action

- If you feel that God is just standing by, waiting to see if you will mess up, meditate on the promise that Jesus took the full punishment for your sins on the cross. Start identifying with your new nature in Christ. You are no longer defined as a sinner but as the righteousness of God in Christ.

———

The Promise of Being Welcome in God's Presence

And so, dear brothers and sisters, we can boldly enter heaven's Most Holy Place because of the blood of Jesus. By his death, Jesus opened a new and life-giving way through the curtain into the Most Holy Place. And since we have a great High Priest who rules over God's house, let us go right into the presence of God with sincere hearts fully trusting him. For our guilty consciences have been sprinkled with Christ's blood to make us clean, and our bodies have been washed with pure water.

Let us hold tightly without wavering to the hope we affirm, for God can be trusted to keep his promise.

—Hebrews 10:19–23

Promise in Action

- If you are tempted to avoid God because you have sinned, go boldly into His presence anyway. Jesus' blood paved the way, and in Him you are welcomed at the throne!

The Promise of Being Chosen by Christ

But you are a chosen race, a royal priesthood, a holy nation, a people for God's own possession, so that you may proclaim the excellencies of Him who has called you out of darkness into His marvelous light.

—1 Peter 2:9 (NASB)

Promise in Action

- If you are feeling insignificant, remember that you are God's own possession. You have an awesome destiny!

———

The Promise of Right Standing with God, Through Jesus

He made Him who knew no sin to be sin on our behalf, so that we might become the righteousness of God in Him.

—2 Corinthians 5:21 (NASB)

Promise in Action

- If you are feeling like a sinner, remember that when you received Jesus, you were taken out of Adam, placed in Christ, and given a gift of righteousness. God made you holy.

———

The Promise That God Will Take Care of You

What then shall we say to these things? If God is for us, who is against us? He who did not spare His own Son, but delivered Him over for us all, how will He not also with Him freely give us all things?

—Romans 8:31–32 (NASB)

Promise in Action

- If you feel lonely, remember Jesus is with you. He's your best friend.

———

The Promise of Christ Living His Life in and Through You

My old self has been crucified with Christ. It is no longer I who live, but Christ lives in me. So I live in this earthly body by trusting in the Son of God, who loved me and gave himself for me.

—Galatians 2:20

Promise in Action

- If you feel like a failure trying to live the Christian life, remember that Jesus will live His life in and through you as you place your trust in Him.

The Promise of a Fresh Start

When anyone is in Christ, it is a whole new world. The old things are gone; suddenly, everything is new!

—2 Corinthians 5:17 (ERV)

Promise in Action

- When you find yourself drawn back to old habits, remember you are a brand-new creation in Christ—and His power is at work in you.

The Promise of Living at Rest

Are you tired? Worn out? Burned out on religion? Come to me. Get away with me and you'll recover your life. I'll show you how to take a real rest.

Walk with me and work with me—watch how I do it. Learn the unforced rhythms of grace. I won't lay anything heavy or ill-fitting on you. Keep company with me and you'll learn to live freely and lightly.

    —Matthew 11:28–30 (MSG)

Promise in Action

- If you are feeling weary, remember that you can go to Jesus anytime about anything. He is your rest!

The Promise of Purpose

For we are God's handiwork, created in Christ Jesus to do good works, which God prepared in advance for us to do.

    —Ephesians 2:10 (NIV)

Promise in Action

- If you are feeling discouraged or aimless, remember that you were created by the hands of God to love and give to others. Walk in the Spirit!

The Promise of Being Made Alive in Christ

For as in Adam all die, so also in Christ all will be made alive.

    —1 Corinthians 15:22 (NASB)

Promise in Action

- If you are worried about death and what comes after, for you or a loved one, remember that through faith in Jesus, you have the promise of the resurrection and eternal life with God.

———

The Promise of Your Unshakable Place in God's Kingdom

Now it is God who makes both us and you stand firm in Christ. He anointed us, set his seal of ownership on us, and put his Spirit in our hearts as a deposit, guaranteeing what is to come.

—2 Corinthians 1:21–22 (NIV)

Promise in Action

- If you're worried about how God sees you, remember that He has set His seal on you as His son or daughter. You're in the family (see also Galatians 4:7, KJV)!

———

The Promise of Intimacy with God

But now in Christ Jesus you who once were far away have been brought near by the blood of Christ.

—Ephesians 2:13 (NIV)

Promise in Action

- If you feel distant from God, remember that you have been brought near to Him through Jesus' sacrifice on the cross. You are not alone!

The Promise of Victory

But thanks be to God, who always leads us in triumph in Christ, and manifests through us the sweet aroma of the knowledge of Him in every place.
 —2 Corinthians 2:14 (NASB)

Promise in Action

- If you feel defeated, remember God leads you in triumph. With God you are a world changer!

The Promise of Blessing

Praise be to the God and Father of our Lord Jesus Christ, who has blessed us in the heavenly realms with every spiritual blessing in Christ.
 —Ephesians 1:3 (NIV)

Promise in Action

- If you feel you are lacking anything, remember that you are blessed in Christ. Jesus is everything you need!

The Promise of Sitting with Jesus

And God raised us up with Christ and seated us with him in the heavenly realms in Christ Jesus, in order that in the coming ages he might show the incomparable riches of his grace, expressed in his kindness to us in Christ Jesus.

—Ephesians 2:6–7 (NIV)

Promise in Action

- If you are anxious and frustrated, remember that God raised you up with Christ and seated you with Him in heaven. His incomparable grace is at work already. Stay seated!

The Promise of Belonging in God's Forever Family

This mystery is that through the gospel the Gentiles are heirs together with Israel, members together of one body, and sharers together in the promise in Christ Jesus.

—Ephesians 3:6 (NIV)

Promise in Action

- If you have been wondering if God's promises are really for you, remember that because of Jesus, you have been grafted in. You share in everything that comes with being a child of God!

The Promise of Wisdom, Righteousness, Holiness, and Redemption

But of Him you are in Christ Jesus, who became for us wisdom from God—and righteousness and sanctification and redemption.

    —1 Corinthians 1:30 (NKJV)

Promise in Action

- If you feel indecisive, remember that Christ is your wisdom. You can make right choices!
- If you feel weak, remember Jesus became righteousness for you. Never forget this gift!
- If you feel unholy, remember you are sanctified because of Jesus. He is your holiness!
- If you've made a bad choice, remember, Jesus is your redeemer. Believe He redeems!

———

The Promise of Certainty Regarding God's Promises

For all of God's promises have been fulfilled in Christ with a resounding "Yes!" And through Christ, our "Amen" (which means "Yes") ascends to God for his glory.

    —2 Corinthians 1:20

Promise in Action

- If you feel tempted to doubt the promises of God, remember that God cannot lie. You can trust Him!

Reflection and Discussion Questions

1. Through her own struggles, Sandra discovered, as she explained in chapter 1, that "guilt and condemnation and trying harder will never deliver us [or] drive us to the longed-for destination of sweet freedom" (pages 8–9). How has the stress of striving for perfection affected your life? your work? your relationships? In what ways do you punish yourself when your expectations aren't met?

2. What would it take for you to get God's unconditional love and unmerited grace, discussed in chapter 2, "settled firmly" in your heart and to know that you can do nothing to earn His favor or acceptance apart from simply believing in Jesus and what He has done for you?

3. It's easy to pray for the big things but refrain from talking with God about the smaller, seemingly insignificant issues. Were you surprised that Sandra wrote on page 29 of chapter 2, "God cares about every-thing that concerns us, and I mean everything. He even cares about that hangnail that is bothering you. His love is so personal"? Do you believe God really does care about every single detail of your life? If you did, how would that change the way you think about God? about yourself? about how you pray?

4. Sandra writes in chapter 3 that the Christian life isn't based on "whether our behavior is good or bad; it's about what we believe" (page 35). Have you ever considered that truth? How can simply *believing right* change how you live and relate to yourself and others

daily? In what areas do you need to focus more on your mind-set and less on your behavior?

5. As Sandra became more aware of the power of God's grace, she started questioning herself, as she describes on page 25 of chapter 2: *"It can't be this easy. There must be something I need to do."* In what ways do Christians complicate grace? How do you define *grace*? Do you live as though grace covers every aspect of your life?

6. For years Sandra misunderstood the gift that Jesus gave us on the cross—until finally one day she realized that instead of viewing "myself as a new creation in Christ with a new nature, I still saw myself as the same person I was before salvation—a sinner" (page 48). What difference does your view of yourself make in your daily life? Do you struggle with seeing yourself as a new creation in Christ? In what ways does reminding yourself of that identity lead you to a more empowered mind-set and help you in areas where you struggle?

7. Instead of constantly struggling and working to be better, in chapter 4, Sandra says that "a life of rest is what God wants for every one of His children" (page 50) and that rather than living by our own efforts, we live in response to the Holy Spirit's leading. Do you believe that's possible? How does that mind-set compare with what you've always thought and practiced? What would a life of rest look like for you? What would change if you began to live in response to the Spirit?

8. Sandra wrote in chapter 7 about how we are changed as we behold Jesus: "When we take time to *notice* Jesus in our lives all throughout the day, we are changed. One way is by *observing* examples of His unmerited favor, anything good that comes into our lives, from getting that parking place at the crowded mall to a promotion at work" (page 98). Think about what you encounter daily that you may have taken

for granted. What things, circumstances, or people might be a visual reminder of God's grace and love for you?

9. In chapter 6, Sandra observed, "Whether we lead millions to Christ or no one at all, He will love us just the same" (page 78). Were you surprised by Sandra's bold statement? Do you believe it's true? Why or why not? In what ways does it make you think differently about your identity in Christ?

10. In chapter 6, Sandra wrote, "Now, am I saying we shouldn't tell people about Jesus? Not at all! But no worries, because once you grasp God's grace, you will naturally be more of a witness for Christ than you ever were by your own efforts" (page 79). In what ways might your ministry toward others be transformed by what God is doing in your own life as you embrace His grace? How might living under grace lead to opportunities in every area of life that living under the law never could?

11. Sandra confessed in chapter 6 that at times she lived as though she were afraid of grace (page 80). What did she mean by that? Do you know of people who live as though they are afraid of grace? How does that affect them? Are you ever afraid of grace? In what ways? How does that fear affect you? your relationship with God? your relationship with others?

12. Does fully living under grace give us a license to sin? Why do some people believe that? Why do some people fear that? How does grace actually keep us from sinning rather than permit us to sin? For people who use grace as the excuse for continuing to sin, what have they misunderstood about the true nature of grace?

13. In chapter 8, Sandra observed that "Jesus never hurried and He never worried, so that means it is possible for me to live without hurrying or worrying" (page 108). What do you worry about most? What would it look like for you to submit your mind and that worry to God and trust

Him as Jesus did? Think about a time when you chose to submit your anxiety to God. How did you feel in that instant? How did things turn out? Do you believe that you drown out the Holy Spirit's leading and wisdom when you choose to focus on your anxiety? What do you miss when you fail to submit to God?

14. In chapter 10, we read, "You and I are not responsible for the outcome. We are only responsible to do our part" (page 137)—to believe in Him. In what areas do you struggle with giving up control and simply believing that God has it handled? Do you believe that, even if the outcome isn't what you want, God still loves you and is working everything out according to His purposes, that His thoughts and plans for you are good (see Jeremiah 29:11)? Why or why not?

15. As you live in grace, you become free to love other people unconditionally. How would that unconditional love affect those closest to you? Who are some people you struggle to love? What would loving them look like to you? How might that love change your perspective toward them?

16. In chapter 12, Sandra defined *success* as knowing that Jesus is with her all the time (page 167). What is your definition of *success*? Has it changed since you've begun living under grace rather than by your own efforts? How have you seen a change since reconsidering what *success* means and looks like?

Author's Note

During 2012, the first year of my journey of grace, I experienced the very definite leading of the Spirit, directing me to the materials I needed to help me get rooted and grounded in understanding true grace.

First, just weeks after God touched me on January 2, I read my mom's (Joyce Meyer's) book *Do Yourself a Favor . . . Forgive.* I was able to forgive myself for all the years of being angry about my own imperfections. This was a critical first step on my journey. See www.joycemeyer.org.

Next, Joseph Prince's books and teachings have also served as a great inspiration to me on this journey of grace. I literally felt like I was in Bible college as I read his book titled *Unmerited Favor.* I learned so much as the veil of legalism was lifted from my eyes, and through Pastor Prince's book I fell deeply in love with Jesus! I wanted to know more, to learn more. I somehow knew this was only the beginning of a most amazing journey. I was certain the Holy Spirit had so much more to download into my heart. See www .josephprince.org.

Next, about ten months into 2012, Andy Stanley, who my husband and I frequently enjoy listening to, taught a series called *Free.* He thoroughly explained God's grace from beginning to end, giving very practical examples and using props to get the message embedded even deeper in my heart. It came just in time, as I had felt I needed further clarity on just exactly what it meant to live in Christ! See http://northpointministries.org.

Finally, there were many inspiring conversations with my husband, my kids, my parents, and some close friends as I was finding my way out of legalism.

Notes

1. I gained much insight on the nature of grace from reading Joseph Prince, *The Power of Right Believing* (New York: FaithWords, 2013), 124–25, 127.

2. Joseph Prince, *Unmerited Favor* (Lake Mary, FL: Charisma, 2010), 76.

3. Andy Stanley, *Free* video series, "Lawless," November 4, 2012, http://wecanbefree.org.

4. My comments here were informed by Andy Stanley's teaching in his *Free* video series, "Staying Dead," October 28, 2012, http://wecan befree.org.

5. Prince, *Unmerited Favor*, 136.

6. Stanley, *Free* video series, "Lawless."

7. Stanley, *Free* video series, "Lawless."

8. Quoted by permission of pastor Jeff Perry at St. Louis Family Church, www.slfc.org.

9. Joseph Prince, "Doesn't Knowing That God Has Forgiven All Our Sins, and Given Us His Grace, Become a License for People to Live a Sinful Lifestyle?" Joseph Prince Ministries, May 20, 2011, www .josephprince.org/faqs/category/questions-about-the-bible.

10. Harvard Health Publications, "The Real-World Benefits of Strengthening Your Core," January 12, 2012, www.health.harvard.edu/healthbeat /the-real-world-benefits-of-strengthening-your-core.

11. Joyce Meyer, *Power Thoughts Devotional* (New York: Hachette, 2013), February 1.

12. Prince, *Unmerited Favor*, 282.

For ongoing encouragement,
please follow Sandra McCollom
on Facebook at www.facebook.com/authorsandramccollom
or on Twitter at www.twitter.com/SandraMcCollom.

Or visit her website at www.sandramccollom.com,
where you can subscribe to her blog.